SURVIVAL OR HEGEMONY?
THE FOUNDATIONS OF
ISRAELI FOREIGN POLICY

Studies in International Affairs Number 20

Studies in International Affairs Number 20

SURVIVAL OR HEGEMONY? THE FOUNDATIONS OF ISRAELI FOREIGN POLICY

by Samuel J. Roberts

The Washington Center of Foreign Policy Research
School of Advanced International Studies
The Johns Hopkins University

The Johns Hopkins University Press,
Baltimore and London

The Johns Hopkins University Press, Baltimore, Md. 21218
The Johns Hopkins University Press Ltd., London

Library of Congress Catalog Card Number 73–8134

ISBN 0-8018-1541-X (clothbound edition)
ISBN 0-8018-1543-6 (paperbound edition)

Originally published, 1973
Paperbound edition, 1973

Library of Congress Cataloging in Publication data
will be found on the last printed page of this book.

CONTENTS

ACKNOWLEDGMENT

I wish to express my profound gratitude to Professors George Liska and Robert W. Tucker for their invaluable contribution to my intellectual development and for their countless personal kindnesses over the years.

INTRODUCTION

This study constitutes an attempt to analyze the historical roots from which Israeli foreign policy has grown. A small state, located in a hostile international environment, Israel has remained dependent —as an indispensable condition for its establishment, survival, and prosperity—upon external non-state sources of support and upon the active and passive assistance during critical stages of its development of a patron great power, both against local and regional antagonists and against a hostile superpower. The state of Israel, drawing upon the historical experiences of the Zionist movement and of the Jewish community in Palestine, has sought to procure the support and sponsorship of a friendly great power, principally by appealing to the national interest of the sought-after benefactor.

A complex of situational factors has structured the Israeli drive for security, power, and position. The foreign policy of the state of Israel is a particular expression of the universal tendency of states to seek to enhance their security position to the maximum possible extent by means of armaments and diplomacy, and of the near-universal tendency of states to pursue their immediate concrete interests with no more than a fleeting consideration of the longer-term interests in a possibly less malefic future international environment a less virile policy might foster.

Israeli foreign policy has at all times been characterized by a scrupulous adherence to the dictates of *raison d'état*. A territorial actor, the state of Israel has repressed all ethical proclivities whenever these threatened to impair the security, power, or prestige of the state. The actual behavior of the state has thus been in conflict with the moral aspirations of at least some prominent Zionist thinkers, as well as with the claims of Israel's apologists.

The perennial traditions of state behavior encompassed in Israeli foreign policy have received a wide range of manifestations as the political entity has evolved from a weak international Zionist movement into a powerful, well-organized movement, sustained by and concomitantly sustaining a growing Jewish community in Palestine, and then into a state, initially weak, bereft of great power support, subsequently a state of increasing power and self-confidence, and finally at present a state, within the regional context, of imperial proportions.

Zionist introversion has intensified underlying factors which would, in any event, have crystallized the Middle Eastern international system around the Israeli-Egyptian conflict as the dominant intrasystemic conflict. Thus the Zionist sense of national separateness from the Arabs has invested the inevitable struggle, arising from the introduction of a technologically advanced state of questioned legitimacy into a system of primitive actors, with an intensity characteristic of ideological conflicts.

The Zionist movement possessed all the attributes of a state—a sense of nationality and national purpose, a reasonably high degree of coherence, a determination to subordinate all values and considerations to the requirements of realizing the state and its principal values—except for a territorial base. All Zionist efforts were directed, in the pre-state period, toward the attainment of such a base.

Before the territory was secured, the Zionist movement, both as an organization and as a community of people in Palestine, acted essentially like a state. It thus sought to achieve its ends by alliances, promises, threats, intervention in the internal politics of other states, and the acquisition of arms. Once the state was established, its behavior differed from that of the pre-state Zionist movement in scope and scale, but not in essence.

The ultimate origin of the Arab-Israeli conflict lay in the attempt of one people to acquire a territory occupied by another people. This territorial combat represents a classic case of an irreconcilable struggle between contending parties over a scarce resource. Political control over the land by one party of necessity deprives the other, if not of its actual physical possessions, then of the indispensable condition for the security of these holdings—political sovereignty.

To this inevitable element of physical scarcity was necessarily appended the dimension of material and resulting psychological imbalance. The introduction of a people, and ultimately a state, possessing technical skills which conferred upon that state an unmistakable military and hence political superiority gravely jeopardized the security (i.e., the real political independence) of the Arab states. The Arabs have so far refused to succumb to the Zionist argument that prosperity would accrue to the Arab world if it accepted Israel and established trade relations. This refusal attests not only to the intensity of Arab animosity toward a state whose illegitimacy they regard as incontestable and whose existence and expansion they regard as a grave threat to their security, weak, undeveloped, and incoherent as they are, but also to an intuitive realization that economic relations with an industrialized state can only freeze their position as suppliers of raw materials. In other words, it could insure their economic subordination to Israel and the establishment of an indirect Israeli imperium.

The disparity in the level of development between Israel and the Arab states, by exciting Arab anxieties about their security position, intensified the Arab animosity which stemmed initially from the grievance they felt at Israel's conquest of Palestine. These two sources of conflict were reinforced by a third: the sense of national exclusiveness manifested by the Jews. A proud and sensitive people, humiliated until the very recent past by foreign rule, the Arabs were incensed by the Israelis' apparent indifference to and disdain for Arab sensibilities and interests.

Peace might have been possible between the Jews and the Arabs of Palestine had the Zionists not insisted upon creating a Jewish state. But this insistence was inevitable, given the meaning of Zionism and the historical experiences of the Jewish people.

SURVIVAL OR HEGEMONY?
THE FOUNDATIONS OF
ISRAELI FOREIGN POLICY

Studies in International Affairs Number 20

A NOTE ON THE FOREIGN POLICY OF THE ANCIENT JEWISH KINGDOMS OF JUDAH AND ISRAEL

I.

There is a significant connection between the modern state of Israel and the Jewish states of antiquity.[1] The Zionist movement, whose creators laid the psychological and diplomatic foundations on which the state of Israel has been constructed, and whose Palestinian leaders have become the political elite of the new state and the practitioners of its statecraft, provides the link between the past and the present. Zionism, particularly since the establishment of the Jewish state in 1948, has developed an intense affinity for ancient Jewish history. While it can scarcely be maintained that the present leaders of Israel delve into the diplomatic history of the biblical kingdoms of Judah and Israel for concrete policy guidance, it is incorrect to hold that the frequent references of Israeli statesmen to the Jews of antiquity, and the national obsession with archaeology, amount to nothing but the craving of a restored people to obliterate the memories of recent humiliations by immersing themselves in the glories of the remote past.[2] Rather, the national absorption in ancient Jewish history reflects something about the attitudes and perceptions and values of the current generation of Israeli policymakers and of the Israeli people. Indeed, the Jewish states of antiquity, like their modern successor, exhibit behavioral patterns

---

[1] There were four Jewish states in antiquity: the unified kingdom under Saul, David, and Solomon (ca. 1030–930 B.C.); the northern kingdom of Ephraim (ca. 930–720 B.C.); the southern kingdom of Judah (ca. 930–586 B.C.); and the Hasmonean state (140–63 B.C.).

[2] Ronald Sanders, *Israel: The View from Masada* (New York, 1966), pp. 16–20.

1

which conform to their fundamental nature as territorial actors.

We propose to consider the relevant highlights of Jewish history up to the destruction of the Temple in 70 A.D. by Titus, in order to obtain a more panoramic view of the traditions of Jewish state behavior and of the interests and attitudes of the contemporary state and its leaders. We shall evaluate the historical experience of the Jewish states of ancient times in the light of three considerations: (1) Zionism, the moving force of the modern Jewish state, is essentially nothing but a revival of the ancient Jewish nationalism, and it may thus be instructive to consider the principal features of the old nationalism and its political manifestations. (2) There are striking continuities in the attitudes and behavior of modern Israel and those of the ancient Jewish states and significant parallels between the international political problems contemporary Israel faces and those its ancient forerunners confronted. (3) Every state does possess an historical memory which affects the decisions of its policymakers.[3]

Jewish nationalism in antiquity, and the behavior of the Jewish people as a political collectivity during the period between the appearance of the Israelites as a differentiated people in the seventeenth

---

[3] The historical memory of a state serves as a fund of wisdom and experience from which the current generation of a state's foreign policy decisionmakers can derive meaningful policy guidance. In the case of a state whose continuity has been interrupted for a long period of time, the identification with the past will, as a rule, be less intense. But the case of Israel is unique in this regard, for the significant political experiences of the ancient state have been preserved in the religious texts around which the life of the Diaspora has revolved ever since the destruction of the temple in 70 A.D. Thus, despite the lack of political continuity, the historical memory of the Jewish people has been kept alive over the centuries.

century B.C. and the destruction of the Temple by the Romans prefigure, in many noteworthy respects, Zionism and the political behavior of the state of Israel, respectively.[4]

The first significant act of the Israelites as a distinct historical entity—their penetration into Egypt beginning in the seventeenth century B.C.—was motivated by a desire to escape from the environment of material scarcity in which they found themselves immured. Similarly, the impulse which moved eastern European Jews of the late nineteenth and early twentieth centuries A.D. to emigrate to Palestine was engendered primarily by the wish to free themselves from the intolerable conditions of economic misery and psychological tension in which they found themselves trapped.

The Israelite tribes which entered Egypt in the second millenium B.C. and those Jews who migrated to Palestine in the twentieth century A.D. did so on the heels of a successful external conqueror: the Hyksos, in the former case, and the British in the latter.

The opportunism of the Israelites of antiquity, who searched for a territorial center in Arabia and Egypt before finally settling in Canaan, foreshadowed the opportunistic quest of the modern Zionist movement for a suitable territorial base in Sinai and East Africa before deciding finally on the self-same region as their historical forebears.

As the Israelites exploited changes in the distribution of power within the premier power in the Middle East in ancient times, so the Zionist movement

---

[4] The seventeenth century B.C. is the date which Simon M. Dubnov, *History of the Jews* (New York, 1967), I: 64, assigns to the Israelite penetration of Egypt. I have relied upon Dubnov for the historical facts of the ancient period.

sought to benefit from the internal difficulties of the principal power in the same region in modern times. Thus the former seized the opportunity provided by the Hyksos' overthrow of the native Egyptian dynasty to enter Egypt, while the Zionist leader Theodor Herzl offered to succor the failing finances of the Ottoman Empire in exchange for a charter to establish an autonomous Jewish colony in Palestine.

Similarly, the Zionist movement followed the path trod by the Israelites of ancient times in seeking to derive territorial gains from the conflicts among the great powers. Thus the Zionists' successful exploitation of the great Anglo-German struggle (World War I) to secure British backing for the establishment of a national home for the Jews in Palestine was an action of the same genre as King Ahab's exploitation of Assyrian pressure on Aram-Damascus to wrest from the latter territory it had previously taken from Israel.

In the same way as the Jews of antiquity utilized the opportunity presented by the unseating of an antagonistic regional hegemon by a benevolent great power to reestablish their territorial position in Palestine—as when they restored Judah under Persian suzerainty following the defeat of Babylon by Cyrus in the sixth century B.C., and when they revived Judean independence in the wake of the collapse of the Seleucid power in the second century B.C.—so in the twentieth century A.D. the Jews seized the chance presented by the toppling of the hostile paramount power of the Middle East to strengthen their embryonic presence in Palestine under the aegis of the triumphant state. Thus, following the defeat of Ottoman Turkey by Great Britain during World War I, they secured British protection for a Jewish national home in Palestine.

Later, they exploited the collapse of British power and will to found their own state with the assistance of the United States.

The Jews, in both ancient and modern times, have, because of their politico-military weakness vis-à-vis other peoples, been compelled to rely upon the good will of the principal decisionmakers of the imperial power of the age for the attainment of their major political goals. Thus the Jews were able, during the reign of the Persian king Ahasuerus, to survive the plotting of their enemies to destroy them, thanks to the pro-Jewish attitude of the ruler. During the period of Roman world hegemony, they were dependent upon the good will of the emperors, who possessed the power to enable them to live in security, as during the reigns of Augustus and Claudius, or who could cause them terrible suffering, as was true during the reigns of Nero and Vespasian. Similarly, in modern times, the ability of the Jews to reestablish their national home in Palestine was dependent upon the favorable disposition of the two principal figures in the British government—Lloyd George and Arthur Balfour. The creation of the state of Israel, as well as its survival, has remained contingent upon the favorable attitude of the American president.

Well-connected Diaspora Jews have played a crucial role in directly influencing the leading policy-makers of the key great powers of the age to adopt a pro-Jewish policy. Thus Queen Esther intervened with King Ahasuerus with decisive effect; Herbert Samuel and Chaim Weizmann played major roles in inducing the British government to issue the Balfour Declaration; Louis Brandeis played a significant role in persuading President Wilson to approve the declaration; and President Truman's intimate friend

Eddie Jacobson procured direct access to the President for Weizmann at a crucial moment.[5]

The Jews of modern times, like those of the remote past, have sometimes suffered from changes in the domestic order of the great powers upon whom they are dependent and from alterations in the balance of power among the great powers. Examples of misfortunes arising for the Jews out of changes in the internal government of great powers would be the overthrow of the Hyksos in Egypt by the Pharaoh Aames, and the accession to the throne of the Seleucid Empire of the fanatical Hellenizing king Antiochus IV in ancient times, and the supplanting of the Weimar Republic by the Third Reich in the twentieth century. Examples of disadvantages accruing to the Jews as a result of shifts in the balance of power among the great powers would be the destruction of the Aramean buffer state by Assyria in the eighth century B.C., which sealed the fate of the northern kingdom of Israel, and the decline of Britain and France and the rise of Nazi Germany in the 1930s, which doomed the Jews of Europe and weakened the evolving national home in Palestine as well.[6]

[5] For the role Samuel and Weizmann played in influencing the British government to approve the Balfour Declaration, see Leonard Stein, *The Balfour Declaration* (London, 1961) pp. 103–30, 137–46, and 378–93; for the influence of Brandeis upon Wilson, see *ibid.,* p. 196; for Eddie Jacobson's intervention with President Truman, see Harry S. Truman, *Memoirs* (Garden City, 1955), II: 160–61.

[6] The belated recognition by the Chamberlain government of the gravity of the challenge posed by the Nazi state led it to adopt a policy which, by its stringent limitations on Jewish immigration and land purchase in Palestine, promised to make impossible the realization of a Jewish majority in Palestine. This policy was embodied in a White Paper issued by the British government on May 17, 1939.

The Israelites of antiquity were forged into an effective political instrument only after a period of enslavement in Egypt and later a series of conflicts with the various peoples of Canaan and its neighbors. Likewise, a segment of modern Jewry has become an effective politico-military force only after centuries of mistreatment at the hands of alien people—principally the Russians and the Germans —and following a protracted period of forcible encounter with the Arabs and the British in the twentieth century.

As the ancient Israelites showed no reluctance about besieging and taking by force a territory occupied by a settled population in the twelfth century B.C. (Canaan), the modern Zionists have shown a similar determination to utilize force, as required, to obtain and secure their chosen territorial habitat in Palestine and to displace or dominate the indigenous occupants of the country. While the Jews of the twentieth century A.D. did not use force in Palestine at the beginning of their settlement, as contrasted with the ancient Israelites' exclusive reliance upon force in their conquest of the Promised Land, the reasons for the Zionists' abstention from the utilization of force in the initial stages of their settlement in Palestine do not, in any sense, represent a renunciation of the use of force, or even a preference (beyond the normal human proclivity to obtain what one desires without resort to what may easily turn out to be a two-edged weapon) for nonviolent means in securing their aims. Rather, the Jews' initial abstention from the use of force is attributable to other considerations: (1) Force, utilizable on a politically relevant scale, was not available to the Jews until they had built up their settlement in Palestine to a substantial degree—until the late 1930s, at the very earliest. (2) Alternative, and, at the same time, more effective instruments were available to the Jews—viz., diplomacy, for securing the protection of Britain for the weak but growing Jewish community, and capital, for the acquisition of land, the establishment of settlements, and the absorption of immigrants. (3) The preeminent position of Britain in Palestine after 1918 precluded the use of force by the Jews and made it unnecessary until the British ceased acting as the protective screen behind which the Jewish community could build up its strength. (4) While the Jews consistently underplayed both the fundamental and unbridgeable conflict of interest which existed between themselves and the Palestinian Arabs and their determination to resort to force whenever necessary to protect their evolution toward a position of mastery within Palestine, they did employ force on a major scale once diplomacy and money no longer sufficed to allow them a steady progression toward their objective of firmly establishing their hegemony over Palestine, with the ultimate intent of creating a Jewish-dominated state. The Jewish state has continued to rely upon force and the threat of force to insure its security.

The principal extrapolitical sanction which provides the moral basis for the modern Zionists' claim to Palestine is identical to that which the ancient Israelites relied upon: viz., the doctrine that Palestine is the Promised Land. As the Hebrew religion provided the Israelites with a divine justification for their strivings for Canaan, so modern Zionism seeks to invest its aspirations for Palestine with a transcendental aura. While the ancient Israelites attained this nimbus through the divine promise, modern Zionism, especially in its predominant atheistic socialist variation, has had to rest content with what-

8

ever sanctity a merely historical connection can invest the territorial imperative. In both cases, the ancient and the modern, the extraordinary nature of the claim serves to justify the same political end. While in the case of the self-sufficient, introverted Israelites of antiquity this need for rationalization was primarily internal, in modern times the requirement for self-justification is external: it is sought in order to influence the outside world to view favorably the claims of the Jewish people.

The survival of the Jewish state as an independent entity in ancient times required the absence of an aggressive regional hegemon, and this condition continues to hold true for the contemporary Jewish state. As ancient Israel's independence was tenuous as long as Aram-Damascus wielded its power in its quest for regional primacy, and as Judea was unable to attain independence in the second century A.D. until the final collapse of the Seleucid Empire, so modern Israel's independence was not established until Britain's position was decisively weakened in the Middle East in the aftermath of World War II. Israel's security would be seriously jeopardized were Egypt to embark upon a meaningful drive for regional paramountcy.

The Jewish states of antiquity benefited from internal political dissensions within hostile neighboring states. Thus struggles between ambitious princes and generals for control of the Seleucid Empire in the second century A.D. diverted Syrian attention from the Judean arena and, even when operations against the Jews were underway, undermined the Seleucid effort. Lysias, the Syrian regent, in 163 B.C. was compelled to lift the siege of Jerusalem when he received word that his political opponent Philip was marching on the Seleucid capital of Antiochia. Similarly, the modern Jewish state has benefited from the competition for power within the Arab world. Thus the conflict between Farouk and Abdullah deprived the Arabs of the opportunity of winning the war against Israel in 1948.

Alignment with a geographically remote superpower to offset threats emanating from great powers situated within or proximate to western Asia has been a central feature of Jewish foreign policy in both ancient and modern times. Thus the Hasmonean monarchy in the second century B.C. sought alliance with Rome as a counterweight to the antagonistic Seleucid Empire, while the modern Zionist movement sought Britain as an ally until the decline of British power and Britain's concomitant transformation into a hostile power, whereupon the Zionists sought the United States for this role.

Israel has traditionally appealed to the premier power of the age with the claim that she can serve as an effective barrier to the hegemonic aspirations of other states in the Near Eastern zone, and with the promise that she will act as a deputy for the superpower within the region. As the Hasmonean regime appealed to Rome by arguing that it would stand as a bulwark against the growth of Seleucid power, so the Zionists of the twentieth century appealed to Britain by insisting that they would perform a valuable role as a counter in the British effort to thwart French aspirations in Palestine, and to the United States, since World War II, by suggesting that Israel will act as a loyal ally against communism, the Soviet Union, and a unified radical nationalist Arab state. In recent years the Israeli appeal has shifted, in response to America's burgeoning self-image as the world's order-maintaining state, to an implicit claim to be a loyal and useful surrogate for performing police duties in the Middle East and economic aid functions in Africa south of the Sahara.

While the Jewish state did, in the second century B.C., conclude the alliance with Rome and, in later years, render loyal service to the Roman state, the Anglo-Zionist alliance, shaky from the outset, soon disintegrated as a consequence of the marked divergence of interest between the two parties. The Israel-American alliance, only now in the process of consummation, promises to be highly rewarding to the United States and to permit Israel, at the same time, a far greater degree of autonomy than under the Roman alliance.

The independence and expansion of the Jewish state in antiquity, in addition to requiring the absence or neutralization of regional hegemons, was also contingent upon the absence of great powers from the regional political arena. Thus the twelve tribes established themselves in Canaan and expanded under Saul and David at a time when internal collapse rendered Egypt innocuous and before Assyria had been able to project its power into the Syro-Palestine zone. Similarly, the Hasmonean kingdom thrived as the Seleucid Empire disintegrated before Rome established a permanent presence in the area. This requisite for the independence and expansion of the Jewish state continues to obtain in the contemporary Middle Eastern international system; Israel has been able to expand only to the extent to which the superpowers have either been committed elsewhere or have stalemated one another in the Middle East.

The sustaining ideology of modern Israel strongly resembles the ideology of the Israelite state of antiquity in several noteworthy respects. Both doctrines contain ethical and social precepts which are limited in their concern to the situation of the internal polity. The ideologies neither prohibit nor limit the use of force in interstate relations, nor do they disallow dispossessing the preexisting inhabitants of the Promised Land. Both the ancient religion and Zionist ideology serve to strengthen the state. The former stresses the need to exalt *Yahweh,* the god who binds the nation together and from whom the Israelite conception of a unique national identity is derived. Later, Judaism, as interpreted by the prophets, enjoins adherence to principles of social justice which will tend to eliminate domestic discord and thereby promote the power of the state. Similarly, and with comparable objectives, Zionism stresses loyalty and the subordination of personal interests to the Jewish state and, in its predominant socialist variant, a fairly equitable distribution of rewards.

The Jewish states of antiquity manifested an impulse toward expansion which the contemporary Jewish state is currently in the process of evincing. The ancient Israelites prior to the establishment of the monarchy in ca. 1030 B.C. occupied territory in Transjordan, despite the fact that Transjordan was not part of the Promised Land of Canaan. During the reign of King David, following the defeat of Israel's enemies by Saul and the consolidation of the state under its first monarch, Israel embarked upon an expansionist course. David extended Israelite power into Aram (Syria), rendering Damascus a tributary state. Finally, under Jeroboam II (781–740 B.C.) Israel reached the apogee of its territorial expansion, extending its sway over all of Aram, including Aram-Hamath on the border of Mesopotamia.

While it may be that Israelite expansion under

David was motivated by the systemic desire to control such predatory people as the Arameans, who would continue to attack Jewish territory unless brought under control and who might in time accumulate sufficient strength to destroy the Jewish kingdom unless checked at an early date, the centrally relevant fact is that Israel expanded beyond its divinely sanctioned boundaries. Ancient Israel's behavior in the realm of international politics was not limited by any religious, moral, or ethical considerations. Like states throughout history, ancient Israel expanded to the extent its power permitted.

In acknowledging no bounds save those imposed by the distribution of power within the international system of which it was a part, and in redefining the legitimacy of its territorial position so as to coincide with the maximal possibilities conferred by the power it possessed, the Jewish state of antiquity anticipated modern Israel. The latter has exhibited a similar propensity to expand in proportion to its power endowment, transcending in the process of expansion the limits "sanctioned" by the 1947 U.N. Partition Resolution. Modern Israel, like the apologists for its Davidic and Hasmonean antecedents, claims that its expansive thrust is engendered by the predatory pressures emanating fom neighboring peoples and, lacking any alternative modality of control, is sanctioned by *necessità*.

The foreign policy behavior of the Jewish state following the restoration of the Jewish people to Judea under Persian auspices foreshadows in several important respects the international political performance of modern Israel. When the Jews returned to Judea from Babylon, they found that a substantial portion of their ancestral homeland had been occupied by neighboring tribes, just as the modern

Zionists who returned to Palestine found the land populated by Arabs. The Jews who returned to their homeland after the victory of Cyrus over the Babylonians proceeded to forcibly eject the foreigners who had settled in the country. The Zionist settlers of the twentieth century A.D. ultimately, through the threat and use of force, secured the departure of the bulk of the Arabs who had taken up residence in Palestine since the destruction of the Temple in the first century A.D. But the Zionists did not, at the outset, attempt to expel the Arabs. For unlike the Jews who returned from Babylon, the early Zionist settlers lacked the power to drive out the aliens. In addition, they did not have permission from their great power benefactor to pursue such a course. Furthermore, the Arabs were able to capitalize upon the existence of alternative great powers; the interest these external great powers manifested in winning the good will of the Arabs induced the British overlord to treat the Arabs with circumspection.

In both periods, the Jews were dependent upon the good will of the leading power of the era for the establishment and development of their position in Palestine. In both instances the respective imperial suzerains possessed a liberal conception of empire which enabled Jewish nationalism to flourish within Judea.

The reestablishment of the Jewish territorial center in Palestine was in both epochs followed by a time of troubles. In neither case did the benefactor great power adequately discharge its responsibility to provide adequate protection for the returning Jews from the hostile actions of neighboring peoples. Thus Persia, concerned principally with establishing its rule over Egypt, ignored the disorders in Judea which attended the return of the Jews, while Britain, increasingly resentful over the costs of its pro-Zionist policy and desirous of appeasing the Arabs, failed to suppress the Arab rebellion of 1936–39 decisively. The upshot was the same in both cases: the Jews, thrust upon their own resources, proceeded to develop both the instruments of war and self-confidence in operating them.

The Jews practiced national exclusiveness during both periods, dissolving all mixed marriages in the early period and maintaining a separate school system and refusing to employ Arab labor on land owned by the Jewish National Fund in the latter period. The two periods appear to have ended differently, however. While the period of Persian domination was followed by a succession of other alien hegemonies, with only a brief period of independence, the mandatory period has been followed by the establishment of a state which is substantially independent and is likely to remain so.

The unfolding of modern Israel's foreign policy reveals striking parallels to the evolution of the ancient state's foreign policy.

Thus the period of consolidation which followed the conquest of Canaan by the twelve tribes and that which succeeded the establishment of the Hasmonean monarchy correspond to the period between 1917 and 1948, when the Jews, having won ingress into Palestine via the Balfour Declaration and the British Mandate for Palestine, directed their energy into the channels of economic development and immigrant resettlement in order to build up the power of the community so that it would in the future be able to constitute itself a state.

The security threat posed the ancient Israelites by the Philistines who invaded their territory shortly after they had established control over most of

Canaan induced the Israelites to establish a centralized monarchy and undertake a successful defensive war. This experience resembles the Israeli war of independence, which was a successful defensive war against the Arab invasion of Israel which occurred immediately after the establishment of the state of Israel. In both instances the "war of liberation" brought the Jews larger territorial gains than they had initially acquired and proved to be not a clearly delineated and limited offensive movement, but rather the first phase of an open-ended advance which in time evolved into an expansionist policy. The tendency to slide from a defensive into an expansive policy manifested itself during the Hasmonean period as well, when the state took the offensive after a brief period of consolidation following a successful war for independence.

Saul's successor David waged a preventive war against the Philistines, who had once again attacked the Israelites. David later extended Israelite power to Damascus. The Davidic expansion roughly corresponds to the period from 1955 to 1967 when Israel, initially to counter the apparent upsurge of Egyptian power, launched two preventive wars. As David succeeded in conquering Philistine territory and in expanding Israelite power in other directions, so modern Israel decisively defeated Egypt in 1956 and 1967 and acquired pieces of Egyptian, Syrian, and Jordanian territory.

David's successor Solomon devoted his reign to self-indulgence and ignored international politics. The consequences of this retreat from involvement in international relations were disastrous: shortly after the close of the reign the Edomites revolted and the Arameans attacked. Finally, the state split into two, the tribes of Judah and Benjamin constituting the kingdom of Judah and the ten northern tribes the kingdom of Ephraim (Israel).

The people of modern Israel are demonstrating a similar propensity toward self-indulgence and the dispossessed Palestinian Arabs toward self-assertion, but it appears likely that the modern state, unlike its ancient predecessor, will be able to sustain its forward thrust. The historical memory of Israel's policymakers is dominated by the remembrance of Munich, and is in consequence keenly aware of the terrible disasters which are likely to befall a state which is remiss in closely monitoring changes in the international distribution of power and in acting to preempt unfavorable developments which are looming ahead. The Israelis appear, for the time being at least, to be in a position to enjoy a high standard of living and at the same time maintain an expansive policy. Indeed, such a policy may ultimately prove to be less costly economically than a defensive posture. The surrounding states are weaker relative to Israel and far less capable militarily than were Solomon's neighbors. Finally, the regional international system has so far enjoyed a greater degree of autonomy vis-à-vis the external great powers than was true in antiquity.

The First, Second, and Third Commonwealths have all displayed the tendency to expand as extensively as the power of the state permits, thereby demonstrating that Israel's behavior has always conformed, in its essence, to the perennial principle of state behavior. In exploiting the collapse of the Egypto-Assyrian-Hittite, Greek, and Arab worlds, respectively, the three Jewish states attempted to insure their contemporaneous and future security and at the same time give full throttle to the desire they shared with all states—the desire to rule.

The situation in which the state of Israel has found itself in the early years of its existence corresponds rather closely in several significant respects with that in which the Hasmonean state found itself following the final overthrow of Seleucid suzerainty in 142 B.C. Thus the state of Israel, like its Maccabee counterpart, is surrounded by a culturally alien people who have a tradition of political hostility to the Jews. Britain, the late regional arbiter, is in a state of enfeeblement paralleling that of the Seleucid Empire in the second half of the second century B.C. The local antagonists of the modern state—the Arab states—are, like the local enemies of the Hasmonean state—the Greek cities—disunited and weak.

Modern Israel, like Hasmonean Judea, has chosen to pursue an expansive rather than a defensive status quo policy, proceeding according to the rationale which emphasizes the necessity of bringing ineluctably hostile neighboring peoples under control by the use of force.

The first ruler of independent Judea, Simon, consolidated his state's position militarily and diplomatically: he fortified key cities and renewed the alliance with Rome. Modern Israel, following her successful struggle against the Arabs similarly reinforced her military position and sought to conclude an alliance with the United States.

Simon's successor, John Hyrcanus, embarked upon a policy of territorial expansion and was followed in this course by most of the later rulers. The expansionist policy was abandoned only when Rome introduced itself into the Near East and became arbiter of the region's destinies.

Like the Hasmoneans, Israel has embarked upon a forward policy. The historical analogy suggests that she will abandon this policy only when the paramount power in the international system assumes direct control over western Asia.[7]

Contemporary Israel appears much less likely to make the fatal error of aligning itself against the principal power of the age than the states of Ephraim and Judah (which resisted Assyria and neo-Babylonia, respectively). Zionist diplomacy has, since Herzl's efforts to induce the German Emperor to act as the protector of the proposed Jewish state, been predicated upon the assumption that it is absolutely essential to obtain and retain the support of the premier power in the international system if a Jewish state is to be established and is to survive. Contemporary Israeli decisionmakers are inclined, within limits, to comply with the demands of the great powers, as was demonstrated by Israel's withdrawal from Sinai during the 1948 war in response to British pressure and by its withdrawal from the Gaza Strip in 1957 in response to American insistence.

The constant pressure on the ancient Israelites from the neighboring peoples—Philistines, Edomites, Arameans, Greek-Syrians, Egyptians, and Romans—involved ancient Israel in frequent warfare. In the predatory international environment of antiquity, allies were untrustworthy: autarchic force alone conferred both success and legitimacy. The contemporary system corresponds in these respects to the earlier one. The ceaseless incursions of enemy guerrillas and the frequent clashes with regular Arab armies involve the Israelis in constant armed strife and create an atmosphere of perpetual insecurity.

[7] For a possible alternative course for Israeli foreign policy, see chapter V, *passim*.

Like its ancient predecessor, Israel has felt compelled, since its birth, to rely for its continuing existence upon its own military forces. The abandonment of Israel by its allies at critical junctures—the British refusal to admit persecuted European Jews into Palestine after the advent of the Nazi regime in Germany; the American proposal of March 19, 1948, for a U.N. trusteeship for Palestine, following its earlier support of Jewish statehood; and the refusal of France to continue supplying arms to Israel after the 1967 war—are modern counterparts of Pharonic Egypt's repeated failures, despite its pledged word to aid Ephraim in the latter's struggle against Assyria, and Rome's failure to render concrete assistance to the Hasmoneans in their conflict with the Seleucid Empire.

In the ancient period, Israel's independence was finally foreclosed by the superpowers of the age. Whether or not modern Israel meets the same fate remains to be seen.

II. ZIONIST FOREIGN POLICY DURING THE PERIOD OF THE BRITISH MANDATE

Zionist activities in Palestine prior to World War I were small in scale. Thus in 1914, after a generation of colonization, the Jewish population of Palestine comprised only slightly more than 10 percent of the total. The *Yishuv* in the same year owned less than 2 percent of the land in the country.[1]

The Zionist movement had from its inception been confronted by strong opposition from wealthy, influential, assimilated Jews in Western Europe and the United States. This opposition persisted during the mandatory period and was a major obstacle in the development of the *Yishuv*.[2] The hostility of the fortunate assimilated Jews of the West was motivated by the fear that Zionism would stimulate anti-Semitism within the countries in which they resided and thereby endanger their position.[3] The obstinate opposition of leading British Jews was particularly harmful to the Zionist cause, as it led the British government to adopt in 1917 a less strongly worded pro-Zionist declaration than would otherwise have been the case.[4]

Leading Zionists, despite their unhappiness with the anti-Zionist stand of many upper-class western European and American Jews, recognized the indispensability of assistance from the Diaspora if the

[1] Alex Bein, *Return to the Soil* (Jerusalem, 1952), p. 47. The *Yishuv* was the Jewish community in Palestine prior to the establishment of the state of Israel.

[2] Albert M. Hyamson, *Palestine, A Policy* (London, 1942), p. 97.

[3] Chaim Weizmann, *Trial and Error: The Autobiography of Chaim Weizmann* (New York, 1949), p. 157.

[4] *Ibid.*, p. 206.

21

Zionist enterprise was to be successful. Like their successors in the government of the state of Israel, who have recognized that Israel is in urgent need of support from the Diaspora, the Zionist leaders during the mandatory period made every effort to enlist the Diaspora's aid. In a speech on September 21, 1919, Weizmann stressed two perennial Zionist themes: the need for economic aid from the Diaspora, and the importance of Diaspora political pressure upon the *Yishuv's* great power protector to secure political concessions for the *Yishuv*.[5]

Zionist foreign policy, for at least the first two decades of the mandate, was shaped largely by Dr. Chaim Weizmann. Presaging the Israeli "doves" of the post-1948 period, Weizmann espoused a policy of moderation and prudence. Such a policy, by avoiding extremism and provocation, would preclude the danger of activating great power hostility and the peril into which such antagonism would place the structure the Zionists were so laboriously constructing.

Weizmann feared that the impatience of the Revisionists: "was constantly pulling the movement toward the abyss."[6] The moderation of Zionist policy during the mandatory period, like the moderation of Israeli policy during the Ben-Gurion, Sharett, and Eshkol governments, was based upon calculations of political utility.[7] As one facet of the policy of moderation during the mandatory period, the Zionists stressed the reasonableness of their inten-

[5] See Weizmann's speech of September 21, 1919, quoted in Chaim Weizmann, *Excerpts from His Historic Writings and Addresses: A Biography,* ed. by Sam E. Bloch (New York, 1962), p. 141.

[6] Quoted in Weizmann, *Trial and Error,* p. 363.

[7] John Marlowe, *The Seat of Pilate* (London, 1959), p. 107.

tions and underplayed the underlying political objective of Zionism.[8]

The gradualist policy which the Zionists pursued until Britain's adoption of the 1939 White Paper enabled the *Yishuv* to absorb a considerable number of immigrants and build up its strength from relatively insignificant levels to a point where it was able to defeat the Arabs militarily and win independence in 1948.

The Zionists (by whom we refer simultaneously to both the leaders of the Zionist movement and the bulk of the Jewish inhabitants of Palestine) never appreciated the authenticity and rationality of Arab anxiety in the face of growing Jewish strength. The Zionists, in their actions and in their interpretation of Arab behavior, refused to take into consideration the fact that the Arabs would feel that their security would be seriously endangered were the Jews to establish a predominant position in Palestine. The Jewish nationalists viewed the Arabs solely as an impediment to the realization of Zionist objectives in Palestine. They had no intention of deliberately hurting the Arabs: on the other hand, they were determined to create a Jewish commonwealth in Palestine. The Zionists, for the most part, hoped that the Arabs would cause no trouble, that they would stand aside and watch passively as Palestine was transformed into a Jewish commonwealth. But the Zionist leaders were resolved that if the Arabs did interfere they would be dealt with.[9]

[8] Weizmann, in 1931, carried this policy of denial to its logical extreme when, in an interview with the Jewish Telegraphic Agency, he stated that he did not consider the establishment of a Jewish majority in Palestine to be a Zionist objective.

[9] See Arthur Koestler, *Promise and Fulfillment* (New York, 1949), pp. 33–34.

While the Zionists' assessment of the Arabs' capacity to interfere with the development of the
Yishuv fluctuated considerably during the mandatory
period, a disregard of Arab apprehensions has remained a salient feature of the Israeli attitude toward the Arabs down to the present day.[10]

The Zionist leadership sought during the first two
decades of the mandate to improve Jewish-Arab
relations or, at the very least, to prevent them from
deteriorating further.[11] This effort contrasts sharply
with post-1939 Zionist policy (and Israeli policy
since 1948), which has more or less ignored the
need to allay Arab anxiety and hostility. A belief in
the tractability of Arab animosity, together with
confidence in their ability to proceed successfully
despite Arab enmity, has led the Zionists since 1939
to abandon the attempt to improve, or at least sta-
bilize, relations with the Arabs.[12]

Opposition within the *Yishuv* to the policy of
moderation emerged at an early date. Even in the
initial years of the mandate, when compelling political realities dictated the necessity of adhering to a
policy of moderation, a militantly uncompromising
faction made its appearance. The Revisionists, in
taking Weizmann to task for his moderate policy,
and in clamoring for the adoption of an aggressive
policy, prefigured the Israeli militants of a later

[10] The Israelis have rather consistently regarded the Arabs
as a less-than-mortal danger.

[11] See Frederick H. Kisch, *Palestine Diary* (London, 1938),
p. 54.

[12] For an eloquent expression by Weizmann of his appreciation of the necessity of alleviating Arab fears of Jewish domination, see excerpts from Weizmann's address to the Twelfth
Zionist Congress (1921), quoted in Norman and Helen Bentwich, *Mandate Memories 1918–1948* (New York, 1965), p.
148.

period. The Revisionists were, as early as the 1920s, psychologically prepared for a military showdown with the Arabs. While they, like all other Zionists, hoped that the Arabs would permit the Jews to create a Jewish state in Palestine without forcefully opposing them, Jabotinsky, like Herzl before him and like the leaders of the state of Israel since, felt no aversion to utilizing force to achieve Zionist objectives.[13] Jabotinsky outspokenly accepted the inevitable truth which most Zionist leaders preferred to ignore: the Arabs were and would in all probability remain unalterably opposed to the cardinal aim of the Zionist program—massive Jewish immigration to Palestine—and would thus have to be fought politically and probably militarily.[14]

Like the militants of a later day, Jabotinsky's position was widely popular within the *Yishuv*. As has been true in the state of Israel, this popularity compelled the more prudent and moderate leaders to adopt a more aggressive policy than would otherwise have been the case. The dynamic of the internal struggle for power, first within the *Yishuv* and then in the state of Israel, has had a significant impact on Zionist and Israeli foreign policy.

The position of the militants with respect to the likelihood of military conflict with the Arabs and with respect to the necessity for this conflict in the event of Arab unwillingness to allow the Jewish community to develop into a state was logically impeccable, given the value system and program of the Zionists, the nationalistic feeling of the Arabs, and the inclination of national communities to seek a

---

[13] See Joseph B. Schechtman, *Fighter and Prophet: The Vladimir Jabotinsky Story* (New York, 1956), II: 324. (Hereafter cited as *Jabotinsky*.)

[14] See *ibid.*, p. 65.

decisive resolution of their political differences whenever it appears possible to do so. In point of fact,
the Revisionist leader differed from his non-Revision-
ist colleagues more in style and bluntness than in
substance.[15] The specific policy positions which Jabotinsky would adopt would depend upon his interpretation of what the political configuration in existence at any given time permitted. They would not be
determined or even significantly influenced by considerations of Judaeo-Christian ethics.[16] In this
fundamental respect Jabotinsky closely resembled
the leaders of the Zionist Organization and of the
official institutions of the *Yishuv*.

While the *Yishuv*, like the state of Israel, for the
most part followed prudent leaders who were animated chiefly by the desire to foster the development
and expansion of the National Home, there did exist
during the mandatory period a small group of Jews
in Palestine who were dedicated to the idea of a
genuine and lasting reconciliation with the Arabs.
These men were willing for the *Yishuv* to make
major political sacrifices so that this understanding
could be achieved. *Brit Shalom*, rejecting the Zionist goal of establishing a Jewish state in Palestine,
advocated instead the creation of a self-governing,
binational state.

The outstanding features of *Brit Shalom* were:
(1) its mere existence, and (2) its overwhelming
rejection by Jewish public opinion.

Future Israeli attitudes toward the Arabs and
toward the question of peace with the Arabs were
prefigured in the negotiations which Ben-Gurion con-

[15] Marlowe, *Pilate,* p. 107.
[16] This is strongly implied in Jabotinsky's address to the
Fifteenth Zionist Congress. See Schechtman, *Jabotinsky,* II:
75.

ducted with them in 1935. The Zionist leader entered into negotiations with the Arabs not to foster
a harmonious and cooperative environment in Palestine as an end in itself, but rather to avoid danger to
the *Yishuv*. Ben-Gurion was driven to negotiate by
the demands of political necessity. As he commented:
"I could not, any more than Weizmann, afford to
shelve the Arab question. In an attempt to find some
common formula for Zionism and its aspirations and
for Arab nationalism, I entered into conversations
with prominent Palestinian Arabs and with repre-
sentatives of Syria, Lebanon, Egypt, and Saudi
Arabia." [17]

As in the period of Israeli statehood, Ben-Gurion
genuinely desired peace. But it was to be peace on
Jewish terms. The leader of the *Yishuv* insisted that
the *sine qua non* for agreement was a Jewish majority
in Palestine. Adhering to a familiar Zionist (and
later, Israeli) line, Ben-Gurion sought to make Zionist political demands palatable to the Arabs by
stressing the economic benefits which would accrue
to them if they acquiesced in the Zionist program.
He proposed the creation of a confederation of Near
Eastern states, with Palestine to serve as its economic and technological center. Arabs throughout
the Middle East, he argued, would derive economic
advantages from the formation of such a confederation.[18]

Actually, as one student of the period has observed, Ben-Gurion's attitude toward the Arabs was
"scarcely different from Jabotinsky's. . . . Like
Jabotinsky, Ben-Gurion recognized the Arabs in

[17] David Ben-Gurion, *Israel: Years of Challenge* (New York,
1963), p. 13.
[18] Barnet Litvinoff, *The Road to Jerusalem* (London, 1966),
p. 213.

Palestine for the adversaries they necessarily were. His policy was to build up a Jewish domination in the belief that the Jewish qualities of dynamism would force the Arabs to concede them the superior role in the country." [19] This attitude toward the Arabs is shared by leading contemporary Israeli statesmen.

The Jewish community in Palestine, from the beginning of the Zionist colonizing effort down to the present, sought to keep its contacts with the Arabs to the barest minimum. This desire stemmed not from any negative feelings toward the Arabs, but rather from an intense introversion. The Zionists were intent upon the development of a self-reliant community which would not in any way resemble the Diaspora life they had led. In their struggle for national regeneration the Jews isolated themselves physically, culturally, and psychologically from the Arabs.[20] The first British High Commissioner in Palestine observed that among the Jews "there are those . . . who sometimes forget or ignore the present inhabitants of Palestine. Inspired by the greatness of their ideals, feeling behind them the pressure of two thousand years of Jewish history, intent upon the practical measures that are requisite to carry out their purpose into effect, they learn with surprise and often with incredulity that there are half-a-million people in Palestine, many of whom hold, and hold strongly, very different views." [21]

The Zionists were, from the first, infused with a sense of the necessity of their work. They believed that they were justified in using any method to attain

[19] *Ibid.,* p. 189.
[20] Maurice Samuel, *Level Sunlight* (New York, 1953), p. 35.
[21] Sir Herbert Samuel, quoted in Stein, *The Balfour Declaration,* p. 94.

and retain access to Palestine for Jewish immigration and land purchase.[22] This conviction persisted
and led to the nullification, in Zionist eyes, of legal or
conventional ethical restrictions upon behavior
which would strengthen the position of the *Yishuv*.
The Zionists, in practice, came to accept that distinc-
tion between private morality and public morality
which states have traditionally recognized.

Idealistic Zionists have continually emphasized
the potential abundance of the material environment of Palestine, stressing the economic development potential of the country and the gains which
would redound to the Arabs as a consequence of the
existence and expansion of the *Yishuv*. But these
Zionists, who hope that a situation of material afflu-
ence will obviate behavior which is, judged by the
precepts of Judaeo-Christian morality, unethical,
have been confronted with an insoluble dilemma
when the posited environment of plenitude does not
in fact exist, when the situation is rather one of
material and psychological dearth and is characterized by competition for scarce resources (particularly, domination over Palestine). In these circumstances, all but the most ethically demanding Zionists have come to accept the primacy of state interest
over ethical behavior.

Zionism, like all other nationalisms, assigns the
first place in its hierarchy of values to the creation
and preservation of the state. All other values are
necessarily subordinated to this primary concern.
When the configuration of political reality does not
allow both the realization of important national
interests and ethically acceptable behavior, the re-

[22] Ben Halpern, *The Idea of the Jewish State* (Cambridge,
1961), pp. 127–28.

quirements of the former ineluctably take precedence over the latter. This demand of the nationalist ethic was accepted by the earliest Zionist settlers in Palestine. It continued to enjoy overwhelming popular acceptance both in the *Yishuv* during the mandatory period and in the state of Israel.

The Jewish inhabitants of Palestine have always had to face Arab enmity. The Arabs during the Ottoman period displayed antagonism toward the religious Jews of the "Old Settlement" and the Zionist settlers as well.[23]

In 1919 the hostility which the Jews aroused among the Arabs of Palestine and Syria was noted by the King-Crane Commission, which observed: "the non-Jewish population of Palestine—making nine-tenths of the whole—are emphatically against the whole Zionist program. . . . It is to be noted that the feeling against the Zionist program is not confined to Palestine but shared very generally by the people throughout Syria." [24] This Arab opposition to the fundamental aims of the Zionist movement was to remain, together with the continuing struggle among the great powers for hegemony in the Middle East, and the drive of Egypt for paramountcy within the Arab world, the principal theme of the international politics of the region down to the present day. It was to greatly intensify the difficulty of establishing and sustaining a Jewish state in Palestine and was to lead to recurrent outbreaks of Arab violence against the Jewish community.

[23] Leonard Stein, *The Balfour Declaration* (London, 1961), pp. 83–84; Sir Ronald Storrs, *The Memoirs of Sir Ronald Storrs* (New York, 1937), p. 359.

[24] Report of the King-Crane Commission, quoted in Jacob C. Hurewitz, *Diplomacy in the Near and Middle East, A Documentary Record: 1914–1956* (Princeton, 1956), II: 70.

The behavioral pattern of the Arabs was established by the Palestine Arab nationalist movement under the leadership of the Mufti of Jerusalem, Haj Amin Muhammed Amin al-Husseini, in the 1920s. This pattern consisted of extreme and unyielding hostility toward the Jews, coupled with a refusal to have any dealings with them. The Arabs rejected the Churchill White Paper of 1922 and the Chamberlain White Paper of 1939. They refused to admit that the Jews had any rights in Palestine. They likewise declined to consider any solution to the Palestine problem short of the establishment of an Arab state encompassing the whole of mandatory Palestine.

This uncompromising attitude has remained the outstanding feature of the approach of the Arab states toward the state of Israel. It has precluded any possibility of a compromise settlement of the Arab-Jewish conflict. Arab intransigence, in conjunction with Zionist determination, has meant that the resolution of Jewish-Arab differences must necessarily occur on the battlefield. This logical necessity, given the Arabs' military inferiority to the state of Israel, has in fact meant that the Arabs have deprived themselves of any concessions they might have been able to extract in exchange for recognizing Israel.

Arab hostility toward the Zionist settlers in Palestine manifested itself during the earliest phase of Zionist immigration. Arab antagonism was, during this initial period, primarily economic in origin. In particular, *fellaheen* resented their dispossession by Arab moneylenders who were eager to foreclose in order to sell the peasants' land to the Jews at inflated prices.[25] With the issuance of the Balfour Declaration and the unmistakable determination of the Zionist movement to exploit Britain's endorsement of Zionism to insure the creation of a viable and powerful Jewish organism in Palestine, the economically motivated anxieties of the Arabs were overshadowed by a more pervasive political fear.

In its report regarding the causes of the anti-Jewish riots of 1929, the Shaw Commission concluded that: "the claims and demands which, from the Zionist side, have been advanced in regard to the future of Jewish immigration . . . have been such as to arouse among the Arabs the apprehension that they will in time be deprived of their livelihood and put under the political domination of the Jews." [26] The Peel Commission, in seeking to explain the origins of the Arab Rebellion of 1936, similarly concluded that the sources of the trouble were: "(i) the desire of the Arabs for national independence, and (ii) their hatred and fear of the establishment of the Jewish National Home." [27] The strongly pro-Zionist Colonel Richard Meinertzhagen agreed that it was the fear of Jewish domination and Arab dispossession which engendered the strong anti-Zionist feeling of the Palestine Arabs.[28]

These Arab fears have been confirmed by the establishment of the state of Israel and the dispos-

[25] Neville Mandel, "Turks, Arabs and Jewish Immigration Into Palestine, 1882–1914," *Middle Eastern Affairs* (no. 4), *St. Antony's Papers*, no. 17, ed. by Albert Hourani (London, 1965), p. 85.

[26] Great Britain, *Report of the Commission on the Palestine Disturbances of August, 1929, Command 3530* (London, 1930), p. 161.

[27] Great Britain, *Palestine Royal Commission Report, Command 5479* (London, 1937), p. 110.

[28] Richard Meinertzhagen, *Middle East Diary, 1917–1956* (London, 1959), p. 73.

session of the Palestine Arabs in consequence of the Israeli victory in the war of independence. Arab national feeling, which grew out of a self-consciousness which was in turn evoked by the presence of an alien people in the Arabs' midst, has only been exacerbated by a conflict in which they have been bested again and again and which their damaged self-esteem compels them to avenge.

Neither the Zionist Organization nor the *Yishuv* paid much attention to the threat posed by Arab hostility until the 1920s, when Arab animosity revealed itself violently, and on a fairly sizable scale, and when the expression of this antagonism appeared likely to lead the mandatory power to renege on its commitments to the Zionist movement.[29] Even then, the Zionists never took the Arab threat terribly seriously. The Zionists' modus operandi has traditionally been to ignore the Arabs and proceed in accordance with their plans, taking care to counter the threat of armed Arab attack by developing and strengthening Jewish military forces. The Zionist perception of Arab animosity has produced a determination to counter it by military self-defense. It has not, for the most part, generated an appreciation of Arab anxieties, or an effort to lessen Arab apprehensions by removing their source.[30]

Arab hostility toward the Jews was, in fact, based upon an understanding that Zionist and Palestine Arab aims were irreconcilable. The Jews and the

[29] Ahad Ha'am was one of the few Zionists who warned in the early period of Zionist colonization that it was necessary to take the Arabs seriously. See Stein, *The Balfour Declaration,* p. 91.

[30] To reduce Arab anxieties by removing their cause would have required the abandonment of the principal Zionist objectives—large-scale Jewish immigration to Palestine, and the ultimate creation in Palestine of a Jewish state.

Palestine Arabs existed in an environment where the realization of one's fundamental objectives would result in the absolute frustration of the other's.[31] Jewish claims to sovereignty over Palestine could never be harmonized with Arab claims to sovereignty over the same country. Partition alone offered a possible solution, at least on a theoretical plane. But on a practical level partition could hardly have proven an enduring answer. The intensity of Arab and Jewish nationalism, the geographical situation of Palestine, the security demands to which this situation would ineluctably give rise, and, finally, the disparity in the level of Jewish and Arab development would have rendered conflict between the Jews and the Arabs unavoidable in any event.

In view of the fact that few Zionists were willing to allow that the Arabs had any rational cause for feeling animosity toward the *Yishuv,* and in view of the impossibility of denying the existence, after the Arab riots of the early 1920s, of powerful anti-Jewish sentiment among the Arabs, and in view of the Zionists' determination to deny that Jewish and Arab interests were irreconcilably opposed and conflict between the two peoples therefore inevitable, the Zionists formulated an explanation of Arab hostility which found the mainsprings of this animosity in external sources. Thus the Zionists laid the blame at the doors of the Arab elite and the mandatory power. The Arab landowners, as the Zionists saw it, wished to distract the attention of the benighted Arab masses from their squalid state and turn their resentment against the Jews. Great Britain, in the Zionist view, was guilty of contributing to Arab-Jewish tensions by constantly yielding to Arab de-

[31] Bentwich, *Mandate Memories,* p. 160.

mands.[32] In accusing these two parties of responsibility for the bitterness of Arab feeling toward them, the Zionists of the mandatory period ignored the claims of Arab nationalism and denied that the behavior of the *Yishuv* played any role in the creation and aggravation of Arab hostility.

The Israeli explanation of the persistence of Arab antagonism echoes that which the Zionists developed during the mandatory period in two fundamental respects: it maintains the denial of Jewish culpability and it retains the claim that the Arab elite arouses hatred for Israel among the Arab masses in order to bolster its own position of social, economic, and political preeminence within the Arab world.

The Israeli explanation differs in two significant regards from that evolved by the Zionists during the period of the British mandate. One relates to the role played by the "imperial protector" in undermining the security of the Jewish community in Palestine.[33] Thus while Zionist leaders criticized Britain in the 1920s and 1930s for failing to perform its protective function properly, and in the 1940s denounced the mandatory power for actively

[32] For the Zionist position that British concessions to the Arabs encouraged Arab hostility toward the Jews, see Kisch, *Palestine Diary,* p. 184.

[33] The role of "imperial protector" was performed theoretically (and, in large measure, in practice, regardless of how reluctantly) by Britain in the 1920s and 1930s and by the United States subsequent to the establishment of the state of Israel in 1948. The imperial protector prevents anti-Zionist great powers from jeopardizing the security of the Jewish community in Palestine, either by means of a direct assault, or by arming the Arabs to such an extent that these dedicated enemies of the Jews are enabled to annihilate the state of Israel (i.e., the imperial protector provides Israel with sufficient arms to offset Arab armament, or else allows her to take preventive action).

assisting the Arabs in their effort to annihilate the *Yishuv,* Israeli statesmen have never openly accused the United States of subverting Israeli security.

This self-restraint with respect to criticizing the United States derives from the fact that Israel is dependent upon the United States in a way the *Yishuv* was not dependent upon Britain in the 1940s. Thus the *Yishuv* was able, in the 1940s, to appeal from Britain to the United States, a stronger and friendlier great power. Israel, on the other hand, must, in the absence of any alternative sponsor, rely upon the good will of the United States. No state can openly castigate the ultimate arbiter of its destiny.

The other factor pertains to the role played by a hostile great power in exacerbating Arab hostility toward Israel in order to further its own political interests. While such a great power existed in the 1930s, Nazi Germany was only marginally involved in the Middle East and was thus not regarded by the Zionists as playing a central role in intensifying anti-Jewish sentiment among the Arabs. The Israelis, on the other hand, have seen the Soviet Union, since 1955, in a very different light. Soviet involvement in Middle Eastern politics has been of considerable duration, magnitude, and intensity. The Soviets have, by equipping the Arab states with modern arms, and thereby nurturing the belief among the Arabs that victory over Israel is possible, contributed significantly to keeping alive Arab antagonism toward the Jews (and have, in addition, created a potentially deadly Arab military threat to Israel).[34]

[34] There were some defections from the official Zionist position during the mandatory period. Thus some moderate Zionists recognized, in the wake of the Arab riots against the Jews in Jaffa on May 1, 1921, that the chief source of Arab hostility

The Zionist case during the mandatory period was built around the claim that the Zionist undertaking in Palestine did not in any way threaten the fundamental interests of the Arabs. Indeed, the Zionists insisted upon the existence of a community of interest between the Arabs and the Jews.[35] The Zionists repeatedly emphasized that their intentions toward the Arabs were entirely beneficent. They stressed that their enterprise had been developed without impinging upon the interests or the property of the Arabs.[36]

The Zionists denigrated Arab opposition by impugning the motives of its organizers and by denying that there existed a community of interest between the Arab elite and the Arab masses.[37] They repeat-

---

toward the Jews was the Arabs' fear of being overwhelmed (Bentwich, *Mandate Memories,* p. 75). Weizmann, on occasion, admitted that Zionist introversion had possibly resulted in the reduction of Jewish energy devoted to reaching an understanding with the Arabs. (See Chaim Weizmann, *The Jewish People and Palestine: Statement Made before the Palestine Royal Commission in Jerusalem on November 25, 1936* [Jerusalem, 1937], p. 23).

Israeli perceptions and claims, like those of the *Yishuv* during the mandatory period, are typical of the perceptions and claims of states in general. States tend habitually to deny that they bear any responsibility for the existence and persistence of a conflict in which they are protagonists.

[35] Thus, for example, the Twelfth Zionist Congress adopted a resolution which asserted: "The determination of the Jewish people to live with the Arab people on terms of unity and mutual respect, and together with them to make the common home into a flourishing community, the upbuilding of which may assure to each of its people an undisturbed national development" (quoted in Nevill Barbour, *Nisi Dominus* [London, 1946], p. 108).

[36] The Zionists denied that their colonizing activities had led them to encroach upon Arab landholdings. They contended that Jewish settlers had in fact cultivated swampy and stony land which the Arabs had considered uncultivable. See David Ben-Gurion, *Test of Fulfillment: Can It Be Achieved?* (New York, 1942), p. 5.

edly denied that the achievement of their objectives would in any way injure the Arabs. They were also steadfast in denying that they harbored either the intention or the desire of dominating the Arabs.[38] Indeed, the Zionists claimed that the activities of the *Yishuv* resulted in an improvement in the Arabs' standard of living.[39] They also pointed out that the Arab elite had failed to improve the living conditions of the Palestine Arab peasants.[40]

The Zionists maintained that they had made serious efforts to reach an understanding with the Arabs, and contended that their attempts failed because the mandatory power, instead of encouraging moderate Arab elements to seek an accommodation with the Jews, appeased the Arab extremists.[41]

In rejecting the contention that they desired to dominate the Arabs, the Zionists ignored the fact that the superiority of Jewish technology, in con-

[37] See Jacobus H. Kann, *Some Observations on the Policy of the Mandatory Government of Palestine with Regard to the Arab Attacks on the Jewish Population in August 1929* (The Hague, 1930), pp. 10–11.

[38] In an interview in 1932, for example, Weizmann stated: "We are coming into Palestine not as conquerors. We are coming into Palestine not to dominate anybody. We are coming to build up Palestine together with the people there . . . Palestine is going to be the common homeland for Jews and Arabs." (quoted in Hyamson, *Palestine,* p. 156). Dr. Abba Hillel Silver similarly denied that the Zionists intended to dominate the Arabs. He insisted that the Zionists' quest for a territorial base for the Jewish people "was to be achieved not through the conquest of other peoples, or through expropriation of other peoples' territory, or at the cost of the happiness and well-being of anyone else, but . . . through our own sweat and blood" (Abba Hillel Silver, "Dreamer and Builder of Zion," *Chaim Weizmann: Statesman, Scientist, Builder of the Jewish Commonwealth* [New York, 1944], pp. 210–11).

[39] See Kann, *Mandatory Government of Palestine,* p. 12.

[40] See *ibid.,* p. 9.

[41] See Kisch, *Palestine Diary,* p. 18.

junction with the *Yishuv's* possession of a far more extensive and sophisticated financial and industrial establishment than the Arabs, would ineluctably place the Jews in a position to dominate the Arabs once the mandatory power disappeared from the scene. Similarly, the argument that a large number of Jewish immigrants could be absorbed into Palestine without displacing the Arab population, as the Jews either developed heretofore uncultivated land or increased the yield of previously cultivated land to such an extent that new settlers could be provided for, ignored the likelihood that the mass immigration of an alien people would generate anxiety and fear among the Arabs and would threaten their psychological if not their physical security.

The Zionists frequently insisted that Arab-Jewish cooperation would be possible as soon as the Arabs accepted de facto Jewish sovereignty over Palestine.[42] They thereby ignored the fact that this was the core issue of the Arab-Jewish dispute and euphemistically attempted to conceal the rationalist and tautological axiom that the Arabs being rational, once the Jews had won the struggle and the Arabs had acknowledged the Jewish victory, then there could be peace on that basis. Thus Ben-Gurion maintained that: "Once the bone of contention of Jewish immigration is removed by clear-cut international decision on the one hand, and assuring Jewish control over their own immigration on the other, there is no serious reason to give up the hope of Arab-Jewish cooperation."[43]

---

[42] This demand was only raised by the official spokesmen of the *Yishuv* in the mid-1930s; before that time, the Zionists stressed the right of each people to develop separately within Palestine.

[43] Ben-Gurion, *Test of Fulfillment,* p. 16.

The Zionists unremittingly contested the assertion that the environment in Palestine was one of scarcity, in which one side would win and the other lose. Lord Grey, in demurring from the Zionist dissent, had in 1923 pointed out that "the Balfour Declaration . . . promised a Zionist home without prejudice to the civil and religious rights of the population of Palestine. A Zionist home . . . undoubtedly means or implies a Zionist Government over the district in which the home is placed, and as 93 per cent of the population are Arabs, I do not see how you can establish other than an Arab Government without prejudice to their civil rights. That one sentence of the Balfour Declaration seems to involve, without overstating it, exceedingly great difficulty of fulfillment." [44]

The Zionist case rested upon the claim that the Jews possessed a moral right to Palestine. This moral right, which antedated the establishment of Arab settlements in Palestine and superseded Arab rights, was confirmed by international law and was invested with a special legitimacy by the dire need of the Jewish people.[45] The Zionist case, as developed during the period of the British mandate, has continued to serve the state of Israel down to the present day.

The behavior of the Zionist movement during World War I conformed to the pattern which Herzl had established more than a decade earlier. Thus the movement was able to derive benefits from the great international struggle by aligning itself with the Allied powers. The Zionist leaders in 1917, like the Israeli leaders today, accepted the realities of

[44] Quoted in Barbour, *Nisi Dominus,* p. 107.

[45] See Ben-Gurion, *Test of Fulfillment,* p. 11, and Chaim Weizmann, *American Addresses* (New York, 1923), p. 22.

power politics, and played the game to the extent to which their resources permitted. As Lloyd George noted: "The Zionist leaders gave us a definite promise that, if the Allies committed themselves to giving facilities for the establishment of a National Home for the Jews in Palestine, they would do their best to rally to the Allied cause Jewish sentiment and support throughout the world. They kept their word in the letter and the spirit." [46]

The Zionists in 1917 traded upon the strongly held belief of key members of the British cabinet that the support of the Diaspora would be an extremely valuable war asset for the Allies.[47] The British government hoped that, in exchange for a declaration of support for Zionist aspirations, wealthy American Jews would come to the assistance of the embattled entente powers.[48] The cabinet also hoped that Russian Jews would exert their influence to keep Russia in the war or, at the very least, would interfere with the central powers' exploitation of Russian resources.[49]

[46] David Lloyd George, *The Truth About the Peace Treaties* (London, 1938), II: 1139.

[47] Stein, *The Balfour Declaration,* p. 6.

[48] Lloyd George, *Peace Treaties,* II: 1122.

[49] Stein, *The Balfour Declaration,* p. 347. The British were also desirous of having Palestine under their control in the future in order to avoid a repetition of the events of 1915, when a Turkish attack against the Suez Canal had been launched via Palestine (see Esco Foundation, *Palestine: A Study of Jewish, Arab and British Policies* [New Haven, 1947], I: 58).

The British came to the conclusion that a strengthened Jewish settlement in Palestine could be employed to defend the flank of the Suez Canal. A final consideration in the British government's decision to sponsor Zionism was the cabinet's belief that the Zionists, who would clamor for British control over Palestine, could be used as a counter in the diplomatic struggle against the French for a predominant position in Syria and Palestine (see Esco, *Palestine,* I: 117).

The Zionists did not confine their diplomatic exertions during World War I to attempting to win Allied sponsorship, as they undoubtedly would not have limited their efforts to trying to secure British and American support during World War II had they possessed diplomatic flexibility, and had the Nazi regime not been bestially and irrevocably anti-Semitic.[50] In November 1914, for example, Zionist publicists in Germany responded favorably to the hint of Kuhlmann, counsellor of the German Embassy in Constantinople, to the effect that he looked forward to the day when the Zionist movement would be within the German sphere of influence.[51]

The Zionists induced the German government on several occasions during World War I to intervene with the Porte on behalf of the *Yishuv*. Thus in late 1915 the German Embassy in Constantinople, acting on instructions from Berlin, to whom the Zionists had appealed, advised the Turkish government to permit the Anglo-Palestine Company to resume its banking operations in Palestine. Shortly thereafter, the German government dissuaded the Turks from carrying out a plan to deport from Palestine all Jews of Russian nationality.

The Zionists benefited from World War I in two ways. In the first place, the war resulted in the removal of an anti-Zionist power from its position of hegemony over Palestine. In the second place, the Zionists were able to collect their reward for the services they had rendered the Allies during the war.

[50] In the early years of independence, the state of Israel made an effort to retain Soviet friendship in order to play the Soviet Union off against the United States. This policy became untenable when the Soviets, for reasons of their own, adopted, shortly after the proclamation of Israeli independence, an implacably anti-Israeli policy.

[51] Stein, *The Balfour Declaration,* p. 212.

Zionism was recognized by the Allies, and Britain sponsored the National Home.

The Zionist movement derived important gains from the outcome of World War II as well. Once again it was able to profit from the enfeeblement and exhaustion of the anti-Zionist regional overlord, which had heretofore thwarted Zionist aspirations in Palestine.

The state of Israel, like the Zionist movement during World Wars I and II, has acquired important benefits from the hegemonic struggle of its era. Thus Israel benefited immeasurably at its inception from Soviet hostility toward Britain (which was an ancillary facet of the unfolding Soviet-American conflict), as this antagonism made possible the delivery of a large quantity of Czech arms to the Jewish forces at a critical moment in the military struggle against the Arabs. Cold war antagonism between the United States and the Soviet Union also redounded to Israel's advantage in that it led to a competitive race to recognize the new state.[52]

While the Soviet Union's arming of the Arabs has not seemed to be advantageous to Israel, it is not the political struggle of the cold war itself, but rather Russian expansionism which has led the Soviet Union to take the Arab states under its wing. It should also be noted that the actual effects of Soviet aid to the Arabs have been radically different from the potential effects. Thus while large-scale Soviet military aid to the Arab states creates a *potential* Arab threat to Israeli security, Israel has been able not only to prevent the materialization of a genuine and immediate threat but to acquire Arab

[52] Domestic political pressures within the United States undoubtedly played a major role in inducing the American government to recognize the state of Israel.

territory as the Arabs, made overconfident and over-hasty by their acquisition of Soviet arms, have rushed prematurely into a military showdown with Israel.

Israel has, like the Zionist Organization during the mandatory period, sought to benefit from the hegemonic struggle of the age. In both Israeli and mandatory times the Zionist strategy has centered on enlisting on the side of the West in the hope of being able to share in the fruits of the anticipated Western victory.

The Zionist enterprise was from the first dependent for its success upon economic aid from the Diaspora and upon the intervention of Diaspora Jews with the governments of great powers which had direct or indirect influence over the course of events in Palestine. Funds for the acquisition and development of agricultural land in Palestine and for the financing both of immigration and of indispensable social services had to come from the outside.[53] Until the founding of the state of Israel, the sole source of funds was the Diaspora. Since 1948 some money has been procured from a benevolent great power —a power whose benevolence, it should be noted, derives largely from the domestic political power of the American Jewish community, which constantly exerts itself in Washington on Israel's behalf.

Dependence on the good offices of Diaspora Jews acting to influence the governments of great powers on the *Yishuv's* behalf has likewise been a salient aspect of the *Yishuv's* historical experience, espe-

[53] Zionist leaders publicly acknowledged this dependence. See, e.g., speeches of Weizmann quoted in Chaim Weizmann, *Dr. Chaim Weizmann, Builder of Facts: Extracts From His Speeches on the Keren Hayesod* (Jerusalem, 1952), p. 5, and in Weizmann, *American Addresses,* p. 46.

cially in times of crisis. Thus, before the British conquered Palestine in 1917 the *Yishuv* was subjected to mass arrests, executions, and expulsions by the Turks. Only financial assistance from American Jewry enabled the *Yishuv* to subsist, and only the diplomatic pressure of the U.S. government, influenced by American Jews, and of the Imperial German government, influenced by German Jews, on Constantinople, induced the Turks to refrain from dispersing and annihilating the Jews in Palestine on the Armenian pattern.

Negotiations between the Zionist Organization and the British government during World War I over the possible adoption by Britain of a pro-Zionist policy revealed to the Zionists the extreme importance of being able to make a credible promise to "deliver" American Jewry.

The vital importance of having American Jewry on its side remains undiminished for the state of Israel today. Financial support from American Jewry is as essential as ever, while the political value of American Jewry's support remains immense.[54]

The activity of prominent American Jews, such as Louis D. Brandeis, in promoting the Zionist cause by winning for Zionism the support of American public opinion during World War I was of incalculable value to the Zionist cause.[55] Indeed, the Zionist movement was oriented toward the United

[54] In 1917 Britain, as the arbiter of Palestine's fate, was the power whose interests American Jewry had to be enlisted to support. Today, with the United States occupying the position Britain once enjoyed, Israel relies upon the American Jewish community to influence the American government to maintain a pro-Israeli stance.

[55] Stephen S. Wise, "In the Authentic Tradition," *Chaim Weizmann: Statesman, Scientist, Builder of the Jewish Commonwealth,* p. 196.

States as early as 1916. This orientation, which was intensified after Britain's adoption of an anti-Zionist policy in the late 1930s, has become the keystone of Israeli foreign policy since the Soviet Union's adoption of an unwaveringly anti-Israeli policy in the early 1950s.

In 1917 Weizmann hoped that Brandeis would be able to persuade President Wilson to exert pressure on the British government to adopt a pro-Zionist declaration.[56] This was the first of several occasions on which the Zionist movement sought to induce the United States to exert pressure on London to act in accordance with Zionist interests. Brandeis was unable to fulfill these hopes, but he did succeed in getting the unsympathetic Wilson to switch from opposition to approval of a British assurance to the Zionists.[57] Wilson's support for the proposed pro-Zionist statement of the British government was of great importance in inducing the British government to issue the Balfour Declaration.[58] Thus, as early as 1917, the critical importance to the Zionist effort of enjoying American backing (and the role which American Jews must play in procuring this backing) was made clear to the Zionists.

Another Diaspora Jew who played a crucial role in the attainment of the necessary prerequisite for the development of the *Yishuv*—British patronage and protection—was Weizmann himself. Weizmann was a masterful and phenomenally successful diplomat, who played an indispensable role in persuading the British government to take Zionism under its protection. His success in convincing British decision-

[56] Stein, *The Balfour Declaration*, p. 197.
[57] *Ibid.*
[58] Weizmann, *Trial and Error,* p. 208.

makers that their nation's interests would be served by supporting the Zionist program enabled the Zionist movement to seize the chance presented by the political upheaval caused by World War I.

The state of Israel's attitude toward the Diaspora and its perception of what it could reasonably expect the Diaspora to deliver were crystallized during the period of the British mandate. Few wealthy American Jews lent much support to Zionism during the mandatory period.[59] From 1922, when the British government announced that immigration to Palestine was to be limited solely by the economic absorptive capacity of the country, until 1939, when it imposed severe restrictions on Jewish immigration, the growth of the National Home was wholly dependent upon the Diaspora (and especially upon American Jewry). The Jews of the Diaspora alone could provide the funds necessary for the development of agricultural settlements and industries which would enhance Palestine's absorptive capacity, and for financing the transportation of immigrants to Palestine and their maintenance there until they could be absorbed into the economy. The land was available: only funds for its development were needed. As the Hope Simpson Report had noted: "Given the possibility of irrigation there is practically an inexhaustible supply of cultivable land in the Beersheba area."[60] That irrigation works were not developed on any sizable scale was attributable to the Diaspora's failure to provide the requisite capital.

Israel's skepticism about the reliability of the Diaspora stemmed from the memory of the Diaspora's

[59] Samuel, *Level Sunlight*, p. 226.

[60] Great Britain, *Palestine, Report on Immigration, Land Settlement and Development, Command 3686* by John Hope Simpson (London, 1930), p. 20.

failure during the mandatory period, and was reinforced by American Jewry's failure to prevail upon the American government to adopt a consistently pro-Israeli stance after 1948.

The attitude of the *Yishuv,* and later of the state of Israel, toward the Diaspora has been comprised, in addition to a large measure of skepticism regarding the Diaspora's will, intent, and reliability, of an element of hostility as well. This hostility has grown primarily out of the feeling that the Diaspora has not fulfilled its moral obligation to contribute its utmost to the upbuilding of the Jewish National Home.

Many Diaspora Jews, fearing the negative impact of Zionism upon their position in their nations of residence, opposed Zionism from the outset. These Jews, primarily drawn from the ranks of the wealthy (assimilated Jews of Western Europe and the United States) did, by their active and passive opposition, hinder the development of the National Home. The advent of the Nazis and their massacre of millions of Eastern European Jews who had not, in Zionist eyes, been transported to safety in Palestine because of the failure of wealthy Diaspora Jews to finance the National Home, intensified the antagonism and deepened the gulf between the Jews of Palestine and those of the Diaspora. (Though it was of course Diaspora Jews who were killed.) An element of accusation has, in consequence, been a constant, if muted, theme in the attitude and relationship of the *Yishuv,* and later the state of Israel, toward the Diaspora.[61]

The launching and success of the Zionist endeavor

---

[61] This accusatory element has remained muted because of the continued dependence of Israel upon the Diaspora.

was from the first contingent not only upon its receiving backing from influential Diaspora Jews but on its finding advocates among important Christian policymakers in the great powers as well. Thus the Balfour Declaration, without which the state of Israel could not have ultimately come into existence, would never have been adopted had it not been for the vigorous support accorded it by prominent British statesmen.[62]

The Zionist appeal to Britain was primarily an appeal to British imperial interests: a Jewish home in Palestine, it was argued, would further a vital British interest—control over the Palestine approach to the Suez Canal.

This kind of appeal was utilized by the earliest Zionist thinkers and diplomats, Moses Hess and Theodor Herzl, respectively. It has continued to characterize Israeli foreign policy down to the present. The Zionists have persisted in the belief that the great power which occupies the position of arbiter of the fate of the Near East can be induced to sponsor and protect the Jewish National Home in Palestine by the argument that the National Home will provide a reliable local surrogate for the imperial power and will serve as an effective guardian of its regional interests. The appeal of this claim, especially to naval-based empires like Great Britain and the United States, which are used to exercising their imperial dominion indirectly and with a minimum of force, has in fact been considerable.

Zionist diplomatic efforts to enlist the patronage of a great power were finally crowned with success

[62] For the crucial role played by Lloyd George, Arthur J. Balfour, Lord Robert Cecil, Sir Mark Sykes, and several other leading British politicians, see Stein, *The Balfour Declaration*, pp. 318–19.

in 1917, when Britain agreed to act as protector of the Zionist enterprise. The existence of a great power protector has been essential for the survival, growth, and prosperity of the Jewish community in Palestine from 1917 to the present. Great Britain played this role from 1917 until the late 1930s, providing the *Yishuv* with a protective shield behind which it was able to build up its strength to such an extent that it was ultimately able to defeat the Arabs and set up a Jewish state, despite intense Arab opposition. Britain was to be succeeded by a rather reluctant United States in performing this role of patron in the 1940s.

Weizmann's efforts to induce Britain to act as great power protector of the *Yishuv* prefigured the efforts of Israeli statesmen to persuade the United States to perform this selfsame role for the state of Israel.[63] In his appeal to British statesmen for support, Weizmann employed the same approach which Herzl had utilized in his negotiations with Britain: he contended that British patronage of Zionism would benefit the international political position of Britain, as a strong *Yishuv* would guard the flank of the Suez Canal. (Promises that Allied support for Zionist aims would redound to its political advantage were made to France as well.)[64] Weizmann

[63] Weizmann always believed that Zionism's future lay with Britain (see Weizmann, *Trial and Error,* p. 165). He hoped that a Jewish commonwealth would ultimately established in Palestine under British auspices (see, for example, Weizmann's address to the British Zionist Federation in May 1917, quoted in Marlowe, *Pilate,* p. 24).

[64] For Weizmann's explicit promise to Britain, which was made in a letter of November 12, 1914, to C. P. Scott, the influential editor of the *Manchester Guardian,* see Weizmann, *Trial and Error,* p. 149. For the Zionist pledge to France that if the Jews were given protection and local autonomy in Palestine by the allies, world Jewry would in return support the

and his colleagues made extensive use of Herzl's technique of utilizing the Diaspora, which would allegedly throw its support to whichever side endorsed and supported Zionist objectives, as a bargaining counter with which to garner the great power support he sought. In securing British support in 1917, the Zionists achieved a spectacular success and demonstrated their ability to engage the predominant power of the Middle East on their side. The leaders of the state of Israel, in procuring economic, military, and diplomatic assistance from the United States at crucial moments, were to display a similar capacity.

Despite the enormous advance for Zionist interests which the Balfour Declaration represented, that document was considerably less emphatic than the draft initially approved by the Foreign Office and the Prime Minister.[65] The first draft had declared that "Palestine should be reconstituted as the National Home of the Jewish People"; whereas the draft adopted on October 4th spoke only of "the establishment in Palestine of a National Home for the Jewish people." The first draft stated that "The Government will use its best endeavors to secure the achievement of this object and will discuss the necessary methods with the Zionist Organization"; while the second called attention to the "civic and religious rights of the existing non-Jewish communities." This latter qualification could be interpreted in a manner which would cripple Zionist work in Palestine.[66]

The reliability of the imperial Anglo-Saxon protector was called into question by this recession.

---

allied powers in their struggle against imperial Germany, see Stein, *The Balfour Declaration,* pp. 288–89.

[65] Weizmann, *Trial and Error,* p. 207.

[66] *Ibid.*

Later British recessions would heighten Jewish mistrust and strengthen the realization among the Zionists that they could ultimately rely solely upon themselves for the attainment of their objectives.

Zionist disillusionment with the British protector, born of the British government's decision to water down the wording of the Balfour Declaration in 1917, grew in the succeeding years. The hostility of the British military, which administered Palestine until June 1920, to Zionism was apparent to the Zionists. The Zionists were disappointed when it became clear that Britain would not, contrary to their expectations, turn unused government-owned property in Palestine over to them. Zionist disappointment was intensified when Jewish immigration to Palestine was temporarily halted following the 1921 Arab riots against the Jews.[67]

When the ban on Jewish immigration was lifted in July 1921, it was with the qualification that immigration was to be restricted to the economic absorptive capacity of the country. The Jews had been treated to the first of several displays of the mandatory power's lack of determination. They had at an early date been introduced to the reality that force could be used to elicit concessions from Britain.

The Zionists received another unpleasant surprise at the hands of their great power benefactor in the following year. On June 3, 1922, the British government issued the so-called Churchill White Paper. This statement of policy seriously undermined the Zionist position in Palestine by excluding Transjordan from the area in which the Balfour Declaration was to apply and by diluting the declara-

---

[67] For Zionist disappointment, see *ibid.,* p. 253.

tion's stress upon the primacy of the National Home.[68]

The 1922 White Paper foreshadowed the later limitations the British government attempted to impose, first unsuccessfully in 1930, and then successfully in 1939, upon Jewish immigration to Palestine. The imposition of restrictions on Jewish immigration in the latter year contributed significantly to making possible the annihilation of European Jewry by Hitler during World War II. The connection between the two events was not missed by either the Zionist movement or the *Yishuv,* both of which received confirmation in the most awful conceivable manner of the validity of Herzl's conception of the basis of international politics and the likely fate of the Jews as long as they lacked a state of their own.

Britain's tendency to renege upon its commitments to the Zionists reached a climax with the issuance of the White Paper of 1939. In July 1937, the Peel Commission had recommended the partition of Palestine into independent Arab and Jewish states.[69] The Arab states joined the Palestine Arabs in bitter opposition to the Peel Commission's proposal. The British government, once again demonstrating its lack of will and its responsiveness to pressure, backed down, repudiating the recommendations of its own royal commission.[70]

[68] Esco, *Palestine,* I: 268. Denying the Jews the right to settle in Transjordan, a large, sparsely populated region, reduced the area available for Jewish colonization, meant an increase in the population density of Palestine, and thereby enhanced the credibility of the Arab argument that there was insufficient room in Palestine for the Jews (see *ibid.,* p. 269).

[69] A portion of Palestine was, according to the Peel Commission recommendation, to remain under British rule.

[70] The British government was, by this time, resolved to appease the Arabs. The Chamberlain government feared that

The *Yishuv* thus found itself abandoned by its great power protector at a crucial moment. Jewry's vital interests were to be sacrificed as British decision-makers came to believe that their nation's interests required appeasement of the Arabs.[71]

This sequence was to recur in the future, with the United States playing the same role Britain had performed during the mandatory period. The United States was to echo the Britain of 1939 in manifesting a willingness to allow Israel's security to be placed in grave jeopardy in order to placate the Arabs and thereby check the growing influence in the Middle East of its great power adversary.[72]

Zionist suspicions of the intentions of the mandatory power were aggravated by the failure of the British administration in Palestine to provide timely protection for the *Yishuv* during the anti-Jewish riots of 1920.[73] As one pro-Zionist observer pointed

---

war might soon break out with Germany, and therefore wished to forestall an Arab uprising in the Middle East (Bentwich, *Mandate Memories*, p. 162).

[71] Britain had attempted to desert the Zionists in 1930. The British government had backed off at that time, however. A combination of factors—the weakness of character of the principal ministers, domestic political pressures, the apparent feebleness of the Arabs, their dependence upon Britain, and the absence of an aggressive, threatening great power on the European scene—dissuaded Britain from jettisoning the Zionists in 1930. The situation changed radically in the late 1930s, with the advent of the determined Chamberlain and the rise of the German threat.

[72] America manifested its nonchalance when vital Israeli interests were threatened in the 1955–56 period, during which time it refused to allow the provision of sufficient arms to Israel to overcome the military disparity between Israel and Egypt created by the Czech-Egyptian arms deal.

[73] The British did not restore order until after a number of Jews had been killed. For Zionist criticism of Britain's failure to act with dispatch in 1920, see David Ben-Gurion, *The Jews in Their Land* (London, 1966), p. 300.

out: "The Administration failed to give protection to an unarmed community who found themselves assailed by a cruel, fanatical and armed rabble." [74]

The Churchill White Paper, which announced that "The Jewish National Home in Palestine is not the imposition of a Jewish nationality upon the inhabitants of Palestine," [75] was regarded by the *Yishuv* as a violation of the Balfour Declaration, which the Jews believed had conferred upon them the right to develop a Jewish state in Palestine.[76] The White Paper thus heightened Zionist mistrust of Britain. Seemingly adopted in response to Arab pressure, the British government's issuance of the Churchill White Paper convinced the Jews that their protector would yield to pressure. Right could not be expected to prevail in Palestine unless it were made efficacious by might. The *Yishuv* quickly assimilated this lesson. In the future it would exert pressure and, ultimately, employ force in order to induce Britain to take the action it desired.

Eight years after the Churchill White Paper the Zionists experienced another "betrayal" at Britain's hands, when the mandatory power issued the White Paper of 1930 (the Passfield White Paper).[77] This statement of policy imposed rigid limitations upon both land purchases by the Jews and upon Jewish immigration into Palestine. Although the Passfield White Paper was virtually annulled as a result of pressure exerted by the Zionist Organization and its allies, the Zionists emerged from the 1929–31 period

[74] Meinertzhagen, *Middle East Diary*, pp. 141–42.

[75] Great Britain, *Correspondence with the Palestine Arab Commission and the Zionist Organization, Command 1700*, June 1922 (London, 1922), pp. 18–19.

[76] Esco, *Palestine*, I: 114.

[77] See Stephen S. Wise and Jacob de Haas, *The Great Betrayal* (New York, 1930), p. xi.

with an intensified mistrust of British intentions and reliability.[78]

Arab anxiety over mounting Jewish immigration led, in 1936, to the outbreak of the Arab Rebellion of 1936–39. The mandatory power failed to supply adequate military reinforcements to suppress the rebellion, with the result that the insurrection persisted for three years.[79] The Zionist leaders were bitterly critical of Britain's failure to fulfill its protective obligation when it did not end the Rebellion with dispatch.[80]

The worst Zionist suspicions were realized in 1939, when Britain issued the Chamberlain White Paper. Zionist resentment, bitterness, and sense of betrayal reached new heights when the document in which the British government renounced its intention of creating a Jewish state in Palestine and announced the curtailment of Jewish immigration, the prohibition of land transfers, and the government's intention of establishing an Arab-dominated independent Palestine state within ten years, was promulgated.[81]

Britain's efforts to whittle down its commitment to the Zionists resulted from the changing requirements of Britain's national interests, as these interests were perceived by British policymakers. This experience of abandonment at the hands of Britain during the mandatory period was impressed upon

[78] Weizmann, *Trial and Error,* p. 380.

[79] Only in 1939 did the rebellion finally peter out.

[80] See, Kisch, *Palestine Diary,* p. 450.

[81] Even Weizmann, whose policy for more than two decades had been based upon cooperation with Britain, denounced the injustice and faithlessness of the British. See excerpts from Weizmann's address to the Twenty-First Zionist Congress, quoted in Leonard Stein, *Weizmann and England* (London, 1964), p. 20.

the consciousness of Zionist leaders who were at a later date to hold leading posts in the Israeli government. Israeli policymakers were thus wary of the possibility that the United States might at some point reevaluate its commitments to Israel in the light of the changing requirements of American national interests. Israeli leaders were taught by their experience with Britain to be prepared for the worst possible development in their relations with Israel's imperial protector. At the same time, they appreciated the necessity of taking great pains to keep the imperial patron favorably disposed.

The Zionist perception of the impotence and uselessness of international security organizations was crystallized at the time of the issuance of the White Paper of 1939. The helplessness the League of Nations demonstrated in this centrally important episode in the life of world Jewry—holding that the 1939 White Paper violated the articles of the mandate, and then failing to do anything about it—prefigured the immobilization of the United Nations at critical moments during the life of the state of Israel. It confirmed the *Yishuv's* understanding that the international security organization should be disregarded entirely in calculating the factors which could be expected to affect the security position of the Jewish settlement in Palestine.

As the 1930s proceeded, the Zionist leadership recognized that Britain, reassessing the international political situation and recalculating the relative importance of the Arabs, on the one hand, and the Jews, on the other, had decided to forsake the alliance Weizmann had played so instrumental a role in forging—the alliance between Britain, an imperial power which required the maintenance of an orderly political atmosphere in the strategic Middle East, and Israel, a dispersed and militarily impotent people, whose claims to an autonomous national existence in Palestine could be realized only under the aegis of a protecting great power.

The Zionists, realizing that British decisionmakers had decided that British interests would best be served by repudiating the Anglo-Zionist alliance and placating the Arabs, hoped that pressure exerted by the United States government and American Jewry would keep Britain from totally abandoning its sponsorship of Zionism. The Zionist reliance upon the United States in its struggle against the adversary great power, which has been a *leitmotif* of Israeli foreign policy down to the present, began with the *Yishuv's* struggle against the 1939 White Paper. The Zionists came to feel, as they carried on their struggle against the White Paper policy, that American assistance could be a powerful instrument in inducing the British government to backtrack.[82] Beyond this, the Zionists recognized that British power was declining, while American power was growing. They understood that the attainment of their objectives would be contingent upon enlisting American support.[83] This realization has remained a basic premise of Israeli foreign policy.

[82] Jacob C. Hurewitz, *The Struggle for Palestine* (New York, 1950), p. 144 (hereafter cited as *Struggle*).

[83] Alan R. Taylor, *Prelude to Israel* (New York, 1959), pp. 37–38.

The period spanning the years 1939–48 was one of bitter disappointment for the Zionists in their erstwhile great power protector, Great Britain. In 1945 the *Yishuv* in general, and most leaders of the Labor Zionist movement in particular, were hopeful that a Labor government in Britain would promote the realization of Zionist aims in Palestine.[1] When the *Yishuv* learned that the British Labor government, in which they had placed such high hopes, would maintain the hated White Paper policy, the Zionists once again felt that they had been betrayed by their great power patron.[2]

Indeed, the *Yishuv* throughout the postwar period experienced nothing but harassment and hostility at the hands of the British. Between 1945 and 1947 the Palestine authorities made every effort to break up the underground Jewish army and prevent illegal immigrants from entering Palestine. After the adoption of the Partition Resolution by the U.N. General Assembly, on November 29, 1947, the British directed all their energies to making it impossible

[1] David Horowitz, *State in the Making* (New York, 1953), pp. 3–4. The British Labor party had long been a staunch supporter of the Jewish National Home. In April 1944, the national executive of the party had adopted a resolution calling for massive Jewish immigration to Palestine, suggesting that "the Arabs be encouraged to move out as the Jews move in. Let them be compensated handsomely for their land and let their settlement elsewhere be carefully organized and generously financed. The Arabs have many wide territories of their own: they must not claim to exclude Jews from this small area of Palestine. . . . Indeed, we should reexamine also the possibility of extending the present Palestinian boundaries, by agreement with Egypt, Syria, or Transjordan" (quoted in Hurewitz, *Struggle,* p. 215).

[2] Ben-Gurion, *Israel, Years of Challenge* (New York, 1963), p. 17.

for the Jews to defend themselves from Arab attacks. The British authorities in Palestine permitted armed Arab irregulars to infiltrate into Palestine from neighboring Arab states; at the same time, they imposed an embargo on arms shipments to Palestine.[3] This embargo jeopardized the very existence of the *Yishuv,* which was poorly armed. (The Arab states, on the other hand, were well equipped with heavy weapons.)[4]

The implacable antagonism of a once friendly great power created a highly dangerous situation for the Israelis in 1948: they were compelled to fight for their lives against an Arab enemy who was formidable because of the military assistance which had been provided him by that power. This situation was to recur in the 1955–56 period, when the Egyptians were able to pose a dangerous threat to Israeli security thanks to the military equipment they received through the good offices of the once pro-Israeli Soviet Union.

Israel became acclimated, by the mid-1950s, to persistent and unyielding hostility from a great power enemy, who jeopardized Israeli security by arming Israel's Arab foes. The Jewish state adapted itself to this condition of its existence in two ways: on the military plane by maintaining a large, highly efficient, costly military establishment, by utilizing the strategy of preventive war, and by acquiring, first from France and later from the United States,

[3] See Ben-Gurion, *The Jews in Their Land* (London, 1966), p. 329.

[4] The British sent military advisory missions to Iraq and Saudi Arabia, supplied heavy arms to Egypt, turned the great stone fortresses they had constructed in Palestine over to the Arabs, and trained, armed, and subsidized the most capable Arab army, the Arab Legion (see Robert St. John, *Ben-Gurion* [Garden City, 1959], p. 130).

vitally needed military equipment; and, on the diplomatic plane, by enlisting the support of the Soviet Union's great power adversary to preclude the possibility of direct Soviet military intervention in the Arab-Israeli conflict.[5] The origins of later Israeli strategy and tactics are, for the most part, to be found in the independence period (1945–49), when Israel practiced military self-reliance, sought to acquire whatever military equipment it could from abroad, and utilized American diplomatic support to counter British enmity.

British antagonism to the Zionist cause found expression in Britain's political and diplomatic actions as well as in its provision of military assistance to the Arabs. Thus Britain rejected the recommendations of the Anglo-American Committee of Inquiry (recommendations, it should be noted, which the Zionists regarded as being so inadequate that they in essence rejected the committee's report themselves).[6] Later on the British government refused to implement the U.N. Partition Resolution. His Majesty's government obstructed the United Nations and frustrated the Jews to the utmost of its ability. Thus it refused to permit the Palestine Commission, which had been charged with the task of preparing for the establishment of provisional Jewish and Arab councils, to enter Palestine until May 1, 1948, two weeks before the expiration of the mandate.

[5] Israeli tactics, which were based upon this general strategy, were to ignore the threats of the antagonistic great power, and the pressure to appease the Arabs which frequently emanated from the American benefactor, while acting decisively in the military sphere.

[6] Britain actually declared that she would accept the recommendations of the committee only if the United States provided military and financial cooperation, and if the Jewish armed bodies in Palestine were disbanded—conditions the British government realized had no possibility of being met.

The mandatory power refused to permit the Palestine Commission to organize local militias to maintain law and order or to evacuate a seaport to facilitate Jewish immigration to Palestine.[7]

The British aided the Arabs and simultaneously failed to protect the Jews.[8] While the British military refused to protect Jewish convoys, British soldiers frequently searched and disarmed them, thereby placing them at the mercy of armed Arab irregulars. The Palestine administration and the British army made every effort to prevent important military positions from passing into Jewish hands during the civil war which raged between the *Yishuv* and the Palestine Arabs (aided by Arab irregulars from other Arab states) from November 1947 to May 1948.[9]

The Israelis understood the tremendous importance to the Arab military effort of British assistance. The overwhelming majority of Zionists undoubtedly agreed with Colonel Meinertzhagen's assessment that "Bevin has done his utmost to assist the Arab League in preventing a Jewish State. Confidently the British Government expected and hoped that the Jews would be driven out of Palestine and Zionism destroyed once and for all."[10]

[7] Jorge Garcia-Granados, *The Birth of Israel* (New York, 1948), p. 270.

[8] David Ben-Gurion, in an address to the Central Committee of the Israel Workers' party on January 8, 1948, observed that: "The Administration is neutral only when the Arabs are the attackers and we the attacked. If it is the other way around—and there have been such cases—neutrality disappears (quoted in David Ben-Gurion, *Rebirth and Destiny of Israel* [New York, 1954], p. 229).

[9] Pablo de Azcarate, *Mission in Palestine: 1948–1952* (Washington, D.C., 1966), p. 57.

[10] Richard Meinertzhagen, *Middle East Diary, 1917–1956* (London, 1959), p. 233.

The experience of seeing their erstwhile bene-factor make every effort to destroy them imprinted upon the minds of the Jews of Palestine a sense of the transience of great power protection, and a sense of its utter unreliability in periods of supreme crisis.

In interpreting British animosity toward Zionism during the postwar period as arising out of the per-ception of British decisionmakers as to how Britain's national interests could most efficaciously be pro-moted, the Zionists remained true to their realist conception of the nature of international politics.[11] The leaders of the *Yishuv* saw in Britain's abandon-ment of the alliance with Zionism another confirma-tion of the conclusions Herzl had reached half a century earlier: states acted in accordance with what they believed were their national interests. Neither the dictates of ethics nor the memory of historical relationships could ever be expected to lead a state to depart from a course of action, if such a course was required by the security, power, or prestige inter-ests of the state. The leaders of the state of Israel were quite correctly to assume that the United States would similarly act in accordance with the dictates of reasons of state. They realistically adopted a strat-egy which sought to advance the interests of the state of Israel by enhancing the state's attractive-ness to a potential great power protector by aug-menting Israel's prestige and power, and hence value, and by substituting a benevolent great power not

---

[11] David Horowitz, for example, believed that Harold Bee-ley, Bevin's adviser on Palestine, was motivated in his un-yielding antagonism toward Zionism by the conviction that the Zionists were damaging Britain's imperial position in the Mid-dle East. See Horowitz, *State in the Making,* p. 38.

committed to a pro-Arab policy for Britain, in the role of Israel's great power guardian.[12]

Zionist diplomacy during World War II resembled that of World War I (and prefigured that of the cold war) in that the Zionist movement attempted to benefit from the hegemonic struggle which the war expressed by enlisting on the Allied side and partaking of the spoils of the Allied victory.[13] As in World War I, the Zionists during

[12] This latter course of action is no longer available to Israel. There is no alternative to the American protector on the horizon, given the massive Soviet commitment to the Arabs, and the inferior power position of any of the non-superpowers. Israel's diplomatic alternatives are thus severely constricted. About all that remains to her is the ability to make a reasonably credible threat to bring about a situation which might well lead to a dangerous superpower confrontation in the Middle East.

Britain's postwar anti-Zionist policy was based upon the Labor party's belief that British interests would best be served by an alliance with the Arabs (Leonard Stein, *Weizmann and England* [London, 1966], pp. 24–25). The Labor government hoped to conciliate the Arab states and conclude treaties with them which would provide for the establishment of joint defense boards and the maintenance of British military bases in the Middle East. The British government was desirous of making the greatest possible concessions to the Arabs on the Palestine issue in order to further its wider policy (Hurewitz, *Struggle,* p. 276). In view of Britain's weakened position and reduced prestige after World War II, in light of the growth of Arab nationalism as a force to be reckoned with, and in view of the fact that world Jewry could render few significant services to Britain after 1945 (with the exception of supporting American aid to Britain, which, in view of Anglo-American ties and the Soviet threat would almost certainly have been forthcoming in any event), the British Labor government was willing to renege on its earlier pronouncements, and adopt a pro-Arab policy.

[13] The unalterably anti-Semitic stance of Nazi Germany deprived the Zionists of diplomatic maneuverability during World War II. They were compelled to support the allies; they could not attempt to play the two sides off against one another as they had during World War I. Similarly, during

World War II argued that Britain would be further-
ing its own interests by accepting Zionist help on
Zionist terms. Thus Vladimir Jabotinsky, who attempted to persuade the British government to form
wholly Jewish military units, because he believed
that the formation of such units would conduce to
the realization of Zionist aims after the war, insisted
that conceding to his demands would serve British
national interests. He contended that the employment of Jewish troops would enhance the credibility of Britain's moral claims in the eyes of Ameri-
cans, as it would assure the United States that the
war was not being waged solely on behalf of the
imperial interests of Great Britain and France. Simultaneously, the creation of a Jewish army would
stimulate pro-Allied activity among the Jews in
every neutral nation.[14]

Zionist leaders, in the time-honored tradition of
Jewish statecraft, formulated their wartime and
postwar political strategy in accordance with their
assessment of the likely postwar structure of power
relations among the great powers. The specific conclusion which the leaders of the *Yishuv* reached was
a guardedly optimistic one: a Jewish state could be
established after the war provided that the Jews
exerted themselves to their utmost, in view of the

the cold war, the firm Soviet commitment to the Arabs after
1955 deprived Israel of diplomatic flexibility.

[14] See Vladimir Jabotinsky, *The War and the Jew* (New
York, 1942), p. 106. Jabotinsky's efforts were supported by
Weizmann, who on December 1, 1939, proposed that the
British government permit the Jewish Agency to recruit a
division of Jewish soldiers to fight on the allied side.

Zionist leaders in Britain also attempted to win the support
of leading British politicians for the creation of a Jewish state
in Palestine after the war (see Chaim Weizmann, *Trial and
Error* [New York, 1949], p. 143, and Hurewitz, *Struggle,*
p. 143).

likelihood that the hostile regional overlord of the Middle East would emerge from the war in such a state of exhaustion that she would be unable to impose her will upon Palestine.[15] The Arabs by themselves would not possess sufficient power to prevent the establishment of a Jewish state.

Ben-Gurion was keenly aware of the growth of American power throughout the world and of the likely international primacy of the United States in the postwar period. Zionist leaders were hopeful that the United States could be enrolled as the great power benefactor of their cause, thereby neutralizing the hostility of that state which might otherwise prevent the emergence of the Jewish state. The United States thus loomed increasingly large in Zionist calculations during the final phase of the mandatory period.[16]

The Zionist, and later the Israeli, foreign policy *Weltanschauung* were decisively influenced by the Nazi holocaust and by the world's failure to respond

[15] See Ben-Gurion, *Israel, Years of Challenge,* p. 17.

[16] Zionist lobbying efforts in the United States were intensified during this period (Alan R. Taylor, *Prelude to Israel* [New York, 1959], p. 55). Even the Anglophile Weizmann inclined increasingly in the direction of attempting to secure and employ American support as the primary means of obtaining Jewish sovereignty in Palestine (Richard Meinertzhagen, *Middle East Diary, 1917–1956* [London, 1959], p. 183). The principal Zionist leader in Palestine, for his part, fully appreciated the decisive shift in power from Britain to America, and was resolved to utilize the new power realities for the benefit of Zionism. As Ben-Gurion retrospectively observed, he "no longer doubted that the center of gravity of our political work in the international arena had shifted from Britain to the United States, which had firmly grasped world leadership and in which the largest and most influential Jewish concentration in the Diaspora was to be found. . . . Hitler would be beaten and destroyed, but the strength of Europe would be undermined and its existence dependent for many years on America's economic aid" (quoted in Ben-Gurion, *Israel, Years of Challenge,* pp. 17–18).

to it in a meaningful way. In particular, the Zionists noted the failure of both the great powers and the Diaspora to mount a major effort to rescue European Jewry. They were thus confirmed both in an ineradicable mistrust of the outside world and in the belief that the preservation of the Jews' most vital interests depended, and would in the future continue to depend, upon the strength and resolve of the Jews themselves. This dual conviction was to result in the permanent freezing of Israeli diplomacy in the mold of *Realpolitik* which Herzl had cast and to lead to the permanent subordination of diplomacy to force and the threat of force as the principal elements in Israel's approach to the Arabs.[17] Of the conviction of the Zionists that the outside world had failed to help persecuted Jews escape from the Nazi danger, there can be no doubt. They were painfully aware that the western powers had, by refusing to open the gates of Palestine to the Jews of Europe, played a major role in the destruction of those Jews. As Weizmann noted in his address to the Twenty-Second Zionist Congress in 1946:

When a disaster fell upon our people in Europe . . . the doors of our Homeland were all but shut in our faces, in spite of many protests of liberal opinion in England and elsewhere, and contrary to the terms of the Mandate . . . the White Paper . . . contributed not a little to our disaster in Europe. . . . For six long years, while the butchery was going on in Europe we continually drew attention to possibilities of rescue. Whenever a

[17] It is probable that the behavior of the Arabs would in any event have compelled Israel to rely primarily upon force. Yet the experience of the holocaust and the world's failure to react did intensify and make certain Israel's predisposition to rely upon military self-help.

new country was about to come under Gestapo rule we asked that the gates of the National Home be opened so that as many as possible of our people might be saved from the fires of the crematoria and the fumes of the gas chambers. Our entreaties fell on deaf ears.[18]

The destruction of one-third of the Jewish people confirmed the Zionists in their conviction that the creation of a state was indispensable if vital Jewish interests were to be protected. It also reinforced their belief that reliance upon legal stipulations or upon the good will of the western great powers was illusory. In short, it steeled their determination to procure and secure a Jewish state by any and every means.

The Zionist belief in self-reliance, which grew initially out of a perception of the moral debility politico-military impotence created among the Jewish people, received its ultimate reinforcement from the apparently inescapable realization that without an independent state Jewry might well be compelled to suffer not only humiliation but physical obliteration as well. The outside world could not be relied upon to come to Jewry's assistance when the annihilation of the Jewish people was at hand. Rabbi Abba Hillel Silver, in laying bare the moral poverty of the western powers' response to the Nazi slaughter, spoke for his people: "The world was silent when a conspiracy of murder was unleashed against a whole people. . . . Here and there one heard a feeble protest, one witnessed a gesture of sympathy. But where was the uproar of outraged

[18] Chaim Weizmann, *Presidential Address at the Twenty-Second Zionist Congress* (Basle, 1946), p. 5 (hereafter cited as *Presidential Address*).

humanity, where was the furious protest of insulted civilization? A spiritual palsy seemed to have attacked the whole world." [19]

The experience of the holocaust created within the Zionist movement and among the *Yishuv* the determination never to allow it to happen again. Weizmann expressed this resolve in his statement to the Anglo-American Committee of Inquiry in March 1946: "I do not know how many Einsteins, how many Freuds, have been destroyed in the furnaces of Maidanek. There is one thing I know: if we can prevent it, it will never happen again." [20]

The Jewish terrorists in Palestine, and later the people of Israel, drew from the lesson of the Nazi slaughter and the circumstances attendant upon it the conclusion that all actions which conduced to the realization of the goal of creating and preserving the indispensable vessel of Jewish survival—the Jewish state—were morally justified.[21] Consequently, the Israeli effort, from the war of inde-

[19] Abba Hillel Silver, "Dreamer and Builder of Zion," *Chaim Weizmann: Statesman, Scientist, Builder of the Jewish Commonwealth* (New York, 1944), p. 211.

For a damning indictment of America's failure to take steps to rescue European Jewry during World War II despite the small cost many helpful actions would have incurred, see Arthur D. Morse, *While Six Million Died* (New York, 1968), *passim*.

For a fuller statement of Silver's bitter criticism of America's failure, see Abba Hillel Silver, *Vision and Victory* (New York, 1949), p. 65.

[20] Quoted in Vera Weizmann, *The Impossible Takes Longer* (London, 1967), p. 202.

[21] The Zionists observed that the holocaust had made little impression upon the Christian world. Their skepticism regarding the utility of appealing to the moral sensibilities of the gentile world was thereby confirmed. (For Zionist comment on the apparent indifference of the Christian world to Jewry's sufferings at the hands of the Nazis, see Horowitz, *State in the Making*, p. 29.)

pendence to the present, has been animated by the belief that the survival of the Jewish people depends upon a determination to fight for their state regardless of all other considerations. As the first Foreign Minister of the state of Israel noted in a speech in 1949: "When the hour came, the Jews knew that their own survival and freedom, in their own country, as well as the fulfillment of the hopes of countless generations, were at stake. In this conviction lay their ability, outnumbered and outarmed, to defend themselves and uphold their independence." [22]

The diplomatic behavior of the American government during the final phase of the mandatory period confirmed the Zionist mistrust of great powers in general, and of the great power upon which Zionist leaders realized they must rely despite their disquiet about its dependability, in particular.

The unreliability of President Roosevelt first gave rise to the Zionists' anxiety about the contemporary and likely future behavior of the United States. Roosevelt's professions of support for Zionism were always ambiguous. While the President issued vague pro-Zionist statements from time to time, he would shortly thereafter hasten on each occasion to reassure the Arabs that their interests would be protected. In February and March 1944, for example, the State Department sent secret diplomatic messages to the governments of Egypt, Yemen, Iraq, Syria, Lebanon, and Saudi Arabia, promising that no decisions on the Palestine question would be taken without prior consultation with

[22] Quoted in Menachem Z. Rosensaft, *Moshe Sharett: Statesman of Israel* (New York, 1966), p. 40.

70

the Arabs.[23] Similarly, several months after the President publicly endorsed the pro-Zionist plank adopted at the 1944 Democratic National Convention, he informed the King of Saudi Arabia that no decision would be made on the Palestine question without first consulting the Arabs.

A major source of Zionist unhappiness with the United States was the memory of America's failure during the Nazi holocaust to render any significant aid to the endangered Jews of Europe. Thus the United States during World War II neither exerted great pressure on Germany to halt the massacre of European Jews, nor upon Britain to suspend the enforcement of the White Paper policy and admit large numbers of Jews into Palestine.[24] Nor did the United States itself display any willingness to admit a substantial number of European Jews.

The diplomatic record of the American government under the leadership of the supposedly sympathetic Truman, while better than that during the war under Roosevelt was sufficiently inconsistent and ambivalent to heighten Zionist fears and suspicions. Thus, after pressing the Anglo-American Committee on Britain and rounding up the necessary votes at the U.N. General Assembly to insure adoption of the Partition Resolution, the United States began to recede from its pro-Zionist position.[25] In the first week of December 1947, the State Department announced the imposition of an embargo on all arms shipments to the Middle East. This action seriously hurt the Jews, as the Arabs were able to

[23] Joseph B. Schechtman, *The United States and the Jewish State Movement* (New York, 1966), pp. 27–28.

[24] See Morse, *Six Million Died, passim.*

[25] Hurewitz, *Struggle,* p. 312.

obtain ample supplies of arms and equipment from Britain.[26]

Two months later, on February 24, 1948, one week after the United Nations Palestine Commission had reported that it would not be able to discharge its responsibilities without armed assistance, the chief American delegate to the U.N. declared that the Security Council was not bound by the recommendations of the General Assembly. The following month, on March 19, 1948, the day after President Truman had seen Dr. Weizmann and had assured him that the United States would continue to support partition, the chief American delegate to the United Nations announced a complete reversal of American policy, stating that the United States believed that "a temporary trusteeship for Palestine should be established under the Trusteeship Council of the United Nations. . . . Pending the meeting of the proposed special session of the General Assembly, we believe that the Security Council should instruct the Palestine Commission to suspend its efforts to implement the proposed partition plan." [27] Eleven days later Warren Austin followed up his proposal with a call for a truce in Palestine. He simultaneously requested a special session of the U.N. "to consider further the question of the future government of Palestine." [28] Whether or not the President knew of Austin's trusteeship plan beforehand is unclear.[29] The *Yishuv*, at any rate, felt be-

[26] Schechtman, *The United States and the Jewish State Movement,* p. 318.

[27] Quoted in *ibid.,* p. 264.

[28] Quoted in Garcia-Granados, *Birth of Israel,* p. 271.

[29] Herbert Feis, *The Birth of Israel* (New York, 1969), p. 53. Feis suggests that the trusteeship plan originated in the State Department and that the President may have forgotten that he had approved it. Feis alternatively suggests that Presi-

trayed.[30] Its American protector had not proven trustworthy.

Although the United States shortly thereafter abandoned its attempt to openly secure the nullification of the Partition Resolution, State Department officials continued to exert strong pressure on Zionist leaders to refrain from establishing a Jewish state. Veiled threats of American disfavor and even of economic sanctions were made.[31] On May 8, 1948, Secretary of State Marshall and Undersecretary of State Lovett capped these efforts when they warned Moshe Sharett that the Jews could expect no help from the United States when they established their state.

American diplomatic action against Zionist interests was resumed in September 1948, when Secretary of State Marshall endorsed the Bernadotte Plan, which would have reduced the size of Israel and would have required the Israelis to allow the Arab refugees to return and be compensated for the property they had lost.[32]

The oscillations of American diplomacy in the period of America's burgeoning involvement in the international politics of the Middle East (1942–48) reflected the pull of conflicting interest groups on the American executive and his desire to satisfy all of them simultaneously, as well as to meet both the

dent Truman may have failed to see how the plan would be construed.

[30] Azcarate, *Mission in Palestine,* p. 27; Zeev Sharef, *Three Days* (Garden City, 1962), p. 30; Arthur Koestler, *Promise and Fulfillment* (New York, 1949), p. 300.

[31] Garcia-Granados, *Birth of Israel,* pp. 284–85.

[32] For the provisions of the Bernadotte Plan, see Folke Bernadotte, *To Jerusalem* (London, 1951), p. 118; for American pressure on Israel to accept the Bernadotte Plan, see James G. McDonald, *My Mission in Israel 1948–1951* (New York, 1951), p. 102.

requirements of the national interest of the United States and the demands of a humane conscience.

On the one hand, there was intense pro-Zionist pressure from the strategically located Jewish electorate and an insistence by professional politicians in both major parties that this pressure be accommodated by the adoption of a strongly pro-Zionist policy. The strength of the Jewish electorate and the efficacy of the pressure it brought to bear was demonstrated in 1944, when a basically unsympathetic President was constrained to adopt a public posture of support for Zionist aspirations in Palestine.[33] In the congressional elections of 1946, as one historian has noted: "The Democrats and their opponents rivaled each other in their advocacy of admission of Jews into Palestine."[34] Keenly aware of the prevailing pro-Zionist sentiment in the United States, as well as of the electoral importance of the Jewish constituency, concentrated as it was in several key northern industrial states, President Truman, to improve the Democratic party's prospects in the crucially important state of New York, on October 4, 1946, publicly expressed his support for the immediate admission of a substantial number of Jewish immigrants into Palestine.[35] Later on the intense pressure of the American Jewish community forced the American government to drop the Austin

[33] The Palestine plank adopted by the Democratic National Convention of 1944 and endorsed by President Roosevelt, called for: "the opening of Palestine to unrestricted Jewish immigration and colonization and such a policy as to result in the establishment there of a free and democratic Jewish commonwealth." Quoted in Bartley C. Crum, *Behind the Silken Curtain: A Personal Account of Anglo-American Diplomacy in Palestine and the Middle East* (New York, 1947), p. 37.

[34] Feis, *Birth of Israel,* p. 34.

[35] Hurewitz, *Struggle,* p. 264.

proposal and led the President, on April 12, 1948, to inform his friend, Eddie Jacobson (and through him, both the American Jewish community and the *Yishuv*) that the United States would recognize the Jewish state if it came into existence.[36] Eleven minutes after the state of Israel was proclaimed on May 15, 1948, the United States government extended it de facto recognition. While the administration was to some extent motivated by the desire to beat its Soviet adversary to the punch, its decision to recognize Israel with great dispatch was engendered principally by the desire to thereby enhance its popularity with American Jews.[37] Later in the year, the President's desire to retain the support of Jewish voters led to another major gain for Zionism. Two weeks before the 1948 presidential election, the Republican nominee accused the Democratic party of failing to honor its obligations to Israel. President Truman responded, on October 28, 1948, by repudiating his Secretary of State's previous endorsement of the Bernadotte Plan and by announcing his opposition to the plan.[38] It was thereby buried beyond hope of resuscitation.

The sensitivity of American presidents to the demands of the Jewish community and their tendency to adopt, in consequence, a strongly pro-Zionist policy has been a major factor in influencing American policy toward Zionism since the administration of Woodrow Wilson. It has remained an invaluable asset of the state of Israel.

On the other side of the coin has been the anti-Zionist pressure which has emanated from the State Department, the army, and the international oil

[36] Feis, *Birth of Israel*, p. 59.
[37] *Ibid.*, p. 61.
[38] *Ibid.*, p. 66.

companies. The U.S. State Department, in the period following World War II, like the British Foreign Office during the interwar period, inclined to the view that the interests of the nation it represents can most effectively be fostered by appeasing the Arabs and leaving the Jews to their fate. The State Department has, since the earliest days of the cold war, formulated its Middle Eastern views primarily with reference to America's hegemonic struggle with the Soviet Union.[39] American diplomats in the postwar period, for the most part, believed that an enfeebled Britain was incapable of retaining her position of supremacy in the Middle East and that the United States had to replace her in that role. The State Department feared that the adoption by the United States of a pro-Zionist policy would alienate the Arabs and drive them into the arms of America's great power enemy.[40]

The Soviet-American struggle for world hegemony, like the British struggle against Nazi Germany, but unlike the Anglo-German struggle during World War I, thus tended to work against Zionist interests.[41] An altered pattern of control over Arab territory (the Arabs now dispose of it, in contradistinction to the Anglo-French control of it in the aftermath of World War I), the intensity of Arab

[39] In 1946, for example, Loy Henderson, chief of the Near East Division of the State Department, told Bartley Crum, one of the American members of the Anglo-American Committee of Inquiry, before Crum's departure: "There is one fact facing both the United States and Great Britain, Mr. Crum. That is the Soviet Union. It would be wise to bear that in mind when you consider the Palestine problem." Quoted in Crum, *Silken Curtain,* p. 8.

[40] H. S. Truman, *Memoirs* (Garden City, 1955), II: 162. This fear has, in large measure, been realized.

[41] Sharef, *Three Days,* p. 36.

nationalism and its inflexible anti-Zionism condemn any power which supports Israel to unrelenting Arab animosity and to the loss of access to the Arab lands. The existence, during both World War II and the cold war, of an alternative great power benefactor for the Arabs (in the "person" of the West's hegemonic antagonist), together with the lack of such an option for Israel, have, in conjunction with the aforementioned factors, led to a severe deterioration of Zionism's diplomatic position in comparison to that which it enjoyed during World War I.

Despite the ambivalent behavior of the United States during the last phase of the mandate, and despite their consequent disenchantment with the state which they had hoped would perform the role of great power guardian, Zionist leaders in the early postwar period realized that American diplomatic and political support, half-hearted and fluctuating though it was, remained indispensable if the Zionist effort were to succeed. The Zionist modus operandi in the period between 1945 and 1948 was to mobilize American Jewry on the *Yishuv's* behalf and have the American Jewish community employ its political leverage within the United States to prevail upon the American government to press the mandatory power to comply with Zionist desires and to forestall and dissolve anti-Zionist activity undertaken by Great Britain.[42] The success of this strategy was very considerable. It was reflected in the decision of the

[42] The "activist" wing of the American Zionist movement, led by Rabbi Silver, was certain that the *Yishuv* would require the assistance of the United States, which he believed was emerging as the greatest power in the world. But the American Zionist leader was sure that the American government would not impose a pro-Zionist policy on the British government unless American public opinion compelled it to do so. See Silver, *Vision and Victory,* Foreward.

American government to pressure Britain into agreeing to the formation of the Anglo-American Committee of Inquiry (and in Britain's yielding to American insistence) and in the decision of the British government, in February 1947, to refer the Palestine problem to the United Nations.[43] American pressure on the Zionists' behalf likewise played a major role in thwarting Bevin's efforts to see that Britain's position in Palestine was maintained.[44]

The Zionists also strove to mobilize American Jews to use their influence in Washington to promote Zionist aims. The American Jewish community was complaisant and its efforts on behalf of Zionism were fruitful. Thus the United States government in 1947 played a decisive role in lining up support for the U.N. Partition Resolution. (It is highly doubtful whether the resolution would have been adopted without this American assistance).[45]

The state of Israel from the beginning relied upon American support (in conjunction with the superiority of the Israeli army over the Arab armies) to assure the preservation of its fundamental interests. Israel was able to defy the United Nations, when compliance with United Nations resolutions would have undermined Israeli security, only when the United States permitted it to do so (i.e., when the United States guaranteed that the United Nations would not impose sanctions). Israel was able to successfully resist the U.N. demand for an international administration for Jerusalem, "thanks to the

[43] Jon and David Kimche, *A Clash of Destinies* (New York, 1960), p. 29.

[44] *Ibid.,* p. 31.

[45] Nadav Safran, *The United States and Israel* (Cambridge, 1963), p. 35.

political strength the Jews in the United States were able to muster."[46]

The supersession of Britain by the United States as the leading power in the world and as arbiter of the fate of the Middle East was a structural development in the international system which was of profound significance for the Zionist movement and, at a later date, for the state of Israel. Of supreme importance was the fact that the United States was able (and willing) to prevent the Jews' great power antagonist from bringing its power into play against them.

Leading Zionists, despite their public emphasis on the necessity for self-reliance, were, like their Israeli successors, fully aware that the success of the Zionist effort did not and had never depended solely upon Jewish resources, as these resources had been, were presently, and would for a long time in the future remain inadequate to the task. The Zionist leadership knew that a great power of imperial dimensions had to be induced to serve as patron of the Zionist cause in order to prevent hostile great powers from intervening against a renascent Israel, and to provide Israel with essential diplomatic and economic assistance. While it is true that the Zionists did not trust great powers, they nevertheless, in the realistic tradition of Zionist statecraft, accepted the ineluctable reality of their dependence upon them.

The Zionist-Israeli realization of the indispensability of American assistance was complemented by an appreciation of the likely limits of that assistance. The Israelis learned before and during the war of independence that their great power benefactor would not send American soldiers to defend Israel

[46] Azcarate, *Mission in Palestine,* p. 183.

and would be averse to meeting any significant portion of Israel's armament needs. The Israelis were thus constrained to turn to Czechoslovakia for critically needed arms in 1948, and to France and Canada in the 1950s and 1960s. In more recent years, the Israelis have built up a sizable domestic arms industry. (For some sophisticated weapons they have been compelled to rely upon the United States, where they have encountered many difficulties.)[47]

To say that the Zionist movement, from 1945–48, and the state of Israel throughout its lifetime have depended upon the good will and financial and diplomatic aid of the United States is tantamount to saying that they have been reliant upon the active assistance of the American Jewish community.[48] The crucial importance of American Jewry to the success of the Zionist endeavor has been fully appreciated by Zionist leaders. Ben-Gurion, for example, was able, in July 1945, to raise the funds necessary to finance the purchase of large quantities of arms for the *Haganah* from a group of prominent American Jews.[49] At a later date during the independence struggle, arms purchased by the Israelis from Czechoslovakia with money supplied by American Jews enabled the Israeli army to defeat the regular Arab armies.[50] Economic subsidies from American Jewry have been indispensable for keep-

[47] In securing Phantom jets in 1971, for example.

[48] The Zionists needed Wilson's endorsement to procure the Balfour Declaration, and the *Yishuv* required financial aid from American Jewry during World War I to survive. Israel, isolated in an unrestrainedly hostile Arab sea, depended upon a sustained, massive commitment from the United States—a commitment which was secured largely through the efforts of American Jewry.

[49] St. John, *Ben-Gurion,* p. 98.

[50] Kimche, *Clash of Destinies,* p. 76.

ing the Israeli economy afloat since that time, while the state allocates enormous sums for arms purchases.

Jewish terrorist attacks against the British began in Palestine in 1943 and were intensified in the following years. The terrorists, who destroyed government property and killed British policemen and soldiers, carried Jewish nationalism to its logical conclusion in the existing political and moral environment. The terrorists believed that in view of the patent ineffectiveness of appeals to the world's conscience, and in view of the higher good the utilization of violence promoted, given the existing circumstances, their resort to force was morally justified.[51] The alternative to resistance (which the terrorists, like the future state of Israel, believed sometimes required the initiation of violence by the Jews), as the extremists saw it, was appeasement; and appeasement would, in the words of the leader of the *Irgun,* lead only to: "the peace of the graveyard, the peace of Treblinki." [52]

The terrorists were convinced that the opposition of both Britain and the Arabs to Zionist aims could be overcome solely through violent Jewish "retaliation." [53] In their belief in the centrality and efficacy of force in international relations, they were in fact doing no more than affirming the view Herzl had propounded half a century earlier. The terrorists' justification for the use of force was the same as that which Herzl had employed (and at the same

[51] For an eloquent statement of this position by a terrorist, see Doris Katz, *The Lady Was a Terrorist* (New York, 1953), p. 189.

[52] Menachem Begin, *The Revolt: Story of the Irgun* (Tel Aviv, 1964), p. 376.

[53] Ben Halpern, *The Idea of the Jewish State* (Cambridge, 1961), p. 43.

time adumbrated that which Israel has invoked since its establishment: the timeless claim of necessity of state).

The terrorist campaign was condemned by the official institutions of the *Yishuv* and by most of the Jews of Palestine, despite the fact that the terrorists' actions aided the Zionist effort enormously in that, by making Britain's position in Palestine untenable, they paved the way for the British withdrawal and a Jewish confrontation with an enemy with which the *Yishuv* was more evenly matched and which it could reasonably hope to vanquish.[54]

The opposition of leading Zionists to the terrorist campaign was based upon both moral and expediential considerations. Thus Weizmann, upholder of the ethical values of Judaism, attacked terrorism by warning that: "These acts which are in themselves morally abhorrent are also barren of all advantage. They expose our hard-won achievements to the prospect of destruction, and they lead us to a bottomless abyss of nihilism and despair."[55]

Weizmann, speaking for the moderates, clung to the belief that Zionist diplomacy would ultimately be crowned with success. The grand old man of Zionist diplomacy failed to realize that diplomacy, which can be successful only as long as credible threats and promises can be made, could no longer be a substitute for force in a situation where Zionism could neither offer Britain anything she needed nor threaten to deprive her of anything she wanted.[56] Prefiguring a later generation of Israeli

[54] Shortly after the founding of the state, the government of Israel adopted a retaliatory policy almost identical to that utilized by the terrorists between 1943 and 1948.

[55] Weizmann, *Presidential Address,* p. 11.

[56] The Zionists could make no believable promises to Britain

moderates, who were antipathetic to the policies of retaliation and preventive war, Weizmann was fearful that the violence of the terrorists would cost the Zionists all the gains they had so laboriously achieved over six decades.[57]

Weizmann, in urging the Twenty-Second Zionist Congress in December 1946, to continue to rely upon the good offices of Britain, demonstrated a failure to appreciate the decline of British power, the probable permanence of the anti-Zionist thrust of British Middle Eastern policy, the intensity of the *Yishuv's* insistence upon an immediate solution to the problem of the displaced persons, and the possibility of inducing the United States to replace Britain as the protector of Zionism.

Weizmann insisted that the *Yishuv* rely entirely upon methods he deemed "ethical" and "Jewish," and totally eschew the use of force. He warned the Twenty-Second Zionist Congress "against bogus palliatives, against short cuts, against false prophets. . . . If you think of bringing redemption nearer by un-Jewish methods, if you lose faith in hard work and better days, then you commit idolatry and endanger what we have built. Would that I had a tongue of flame, the strength of prophets, to warn

---

until British statesmen came around to Colonel Meinertzhagen's view that Israel could serve as an effective British surrogate in the Middle East. The Zionists could make no credible threats as the United States, acting under the imperatives of the cold war, was bound to rescue Britain from economic disaster.

[57] The man who had secured the Balfour Declaration became obsolescent when intense Arab nationalism, deferred to by a Britain terrified of losing its position in the Middle East by offending the Arabs, rendered the achievement of Zionist aims by peaceful methods impossible. As the Zionist movement shifted, in the post-Nazi era, from reliance upon diplomacy to reliance upon force, Weizmann lost his central position.

you against the paths of Babylon and Egypt. 'Zion shall be redeemed in Judgment'—and not by any other means." [58]

Weizmann's insistence that diplomatic tools only be employed to secure the creation of a Jewish state derived from a fastidious inability to follow the dictates of Jewish nationalism to their logical and, given the environment of scarcity which existed in Palestine, their inevitable conclusion. Unfortunately for Weizmann's ethical sensibilities, the use of force by both the *Yishuv* prior to May 15, 1948, and by the state of Israel since, was essential for the establishment and maintenance of the state of Israel.

The new Zionist course was promulgated at an Extraordinary Zionist Conference held at the Biltmore Hotel in New York City in May 1942. The program which this conference adopted demanded that: "the gates of Palestine be opened; that the Jewish Agency be vested with control of immigration into Palestine and the necessary authority for upbuilding the country . . . and that Palestine be established as a Jewish Commonwealth integrated in the structure of the democratic world." [59]

While most of the Jewish inhabitants of Palestine accepted a program which called for the establishment of a Jewish state in part of Palestine, some demanded the creation of a Jewish state which would occupy both banks of the Jordan. A third group opposed the Biltmore Program, advocating instead the creation of a binational state. The binationalists desired to secure Arab consent to and participation in the state which would ultimately be established in

[58] Quoted in Vera Weizmann, *The Impossible,* p. 213.
[59] Quoted in Schechtman, *The United States and the Jewish State Movement,* p. 61.

Palestine.[60] Like the Revisionists, the binationalists remained a minority within the *Yishuv*.

The division of Israeli opinion after 1948 mirrored that of the *Yishuv* during the final phase of the mandatory era in several significant respects. Thus the bulk of Israeli opinion, like that of the *Yishuv*, embraced a relatively moderate viewpoint, while both before 1948 and afterward a sizable body of opinion adopted a more extreme and militant position which during periods of stress was of increased attractiveness to a substantial section of the majority. In both periods the existence and appeal of a militant alternative, represented by a politically potent organization, had a tendency to push the leaders of "moderate" opinion toward a more aggressive stance. Both before 1948 and subsequently, there existed within the Jewish community in Palestine a small, impotent minority which was sympathetic to Arab feelings and wished the *Yishuv* to pursue a conciliatory policy toward the Arabs.

Zionist demands during the final phase of the mandatory period, like Israeli demands after 1948, tended to escalate as: (1) The international political environment and the balance of forces within Palestine and the Middle East seemed to offer more favorable prospects for the realization of Jewish demands; and (2) as the Jews suffered intensified physical and psychological attacks from the outside (the Nazi holocaust, the 1948 Arab attack, and, in the post-independence period, the rising tempo of Arab military preparations), they resolved to secure protection for themselves against a recurrence of physical onslaughts by achieving more solid security guarantees.

[60] Halpern, *Idea of the Jewish State,* p. 41.

The Zionist movement was, during the final years of the mandate, divided by a conflict over the policy to pursue toward the Arabs and toward the outside world. This controversy was to continue after 1948, with hard-liners generally carrying the day against the advocates of a more conciliatory policy.

This outcome was foreshadowed in the 1945–48 period by the triumph of the activists. David Ben-Gurion, whose political position within the *Yishuv* was preeminent, after 1945 abandoned the evolutionary approach he had previously advocated and adopted a more militant line. This switch resulted from the Zionist leader's calculation as to what the Zionist movement could realistically expect to achieve in the postwar world. Ben-Gurion considered the political situation which confronted the *Yishuv* at the close of World War II—Britain's apparent decision to maintain her pro-Arab policy, the desperate plight of the remnants of European Jewry, the *Yishuv's* fury at Britain for continuing to bar Jewish immigration to Palestine, the weakness and relative mildness of the British (which suggested that a policy of vigorous resistance was likely to be successful), the growth of American power and of American participation in Middle Eastern affairs, and the evident possibility of inducing the United States to sponsor the establishment of a Jewish state in Palestine—and came to the conclusion that the policy of gradualism should be superseded by a more forceful policy.

Ben-Gurion's policy during the final phase of the mandatory period, anticipating that of the state of Israel, was built upon two foundations: diplomacy, and force. The Zionist leader was aware of the possibility of attaining certain objectives through diplomatic means. At the same time, he was cognizant of the necessity of relying upon force, which he realized it would ultimately be necessary to employ.

Ben-Gurion was convinced of the ineluctability of armed conflict in Palestine. Like the terrorists, he was resolved that the *Yishuv* should stake everything on the effort to achieve statehood. Ben-Gurion believed that only a Jewish state could assure the security and well-being of the *Yishuv*. Guarantees were meaningless; living as a minority under Arab rule would be both physically dangerous and psychologically intolerable. This conviction and the determination to fight to the death for a Jewish state to which it gave rise sprang from a consciousness of the likely fate of the Jews in the absence of a state of their own—a consciousness which was molded by the Jews' memory of their historical catastrophe.[61]

The behavior of the *Yishuv's* great power enemy and of its regional adversaries, in the 1945–48 period, was the determining factor in deciding the issue of the foreign policy debate within the *Yishuv*, as was to be the case at crucial moments in Israel's history as well. The antagonistic, menacing, and intransigent behavior of Israel's foes has seemed to the Jews to dictate a resort to force on their part in order to survive. The overt hostility of the Jews' great power and regional foes has, time and again, led to the triumph of the militants within the *Yishuv* and within the state of Israel, not only as a consequence of the rational calculation that only through threatening and using force can Israel defeat those who threaten to destroy her, but indirectly, through influencing the struggle for power within Israel. Specifically, the behavior of Israel's antagonists, by strengthening the appeal of the extremists to Israeli

[61] See Horowitz, *State in the Making*, pp. 111–12.

public opinion, has induced the Israeli government to seek to offset the extremists' growing popularity by adopting a militant policy itself.[62]

Thus, in the autumn of 1945, when it became clear that the British Labor government would adhere to the anti-Zionist policy established by the Chamberlain White Paper, the *Haganah* ceased cooperating with the Palestine administration against the Jewish terrorists.[63]

Britain's behavior following the conclusion of World War II crystallized Jewish animosity and confirmed the *Yishuv* in the belief that it would be necessary to use force if fundamental Zionist aims were to be achieved. (When the British government decided to detain illegal immigrants on Cyprus, for example, rather than in Palestine, the *Yishuv* was overwhelmed by feelings of "fury and helplessness." [64])

Most Jews in Palestine were, at the end of World War II, in favor of pushing ahead with the Zionist program, despite the existence of fierce Arab and adversary great power opposition. Opinion in the *Yishuv* was favorable to simultaneously seeking to

[62] The *Irgun,* during the final phase of the mandatory period, enjoyed widespread sympathy as a consequence of its attacks on British forces, and the leading figures within the official institutions of the *Yishuv* feared that the influence of the terrorists within the *Yishuv* would grow if the Zionist establishment confined itself to verbal protests against British policies. See Theodore Huebner and Carl Hermann Voss, *This Is Israel* (New York, 1956), p. 88.

[63] The *Haganah,* following the assassination of Lord Moyne, British minister of state for the Middle East, in October 1944, had instituted a policy of cooperation with the British police against the terrorists. The Zionist leaders were fearful that a continuation of terrorist activities would cause world opinion to turn against Zionism. See Koestler, *Promise and Fulfillment,* p. 95.

[64] Horowitz, *State in the Making,* p. 119.

enlist the United States as the great power patron of the Zionist program. The Zionist Organization proceeded with this two-pronged policy between 1945 and 1948, and the state of Israel has continued it down to the present.[65]

The Zionist leadership in the period from 1945–48 continued to cherish the time-honored Zionist belief that the Arabs did not possess sufficient power to prevent the attainment of the principal Zionist objectives. At the same time, Zionist leaders expected and publicly expressed their confidence that the Arabs would ultimately acquiesce in the *fait accompli* which Zionist energy and determination would produce.[66] The enduring Zionist belief that the Arabs will ultimately accede to a reality which Jewish determination and strength has imposed, while reflecting the *Realpolitik* tradition of Zionist diplomacy, is curiously oblivious to the possibility that the motive power behind Zionist success—the intense and irrational (given the configuration of forces) determination to struggle on indefinitely against apparently insurmountable obstacles—may similarly inspire the Arabs and counteract a "rational" tendency to accept a settlement imposed by superior Jewish arms and diplomacy.

The Arabs consistently expressed what was an

[65] Ben-Gurion recognized that Arab and British opposition to the Zionist program was likely to persist. In asserting that: "No political opposition on the part of the Arabs, no terrorist intimidation, no restrictions of a morally and legally invalid White Paper will prevent Jews from getting back to the Land of Israel," he expressed the *Yishuv's* determination to ignore that opposition (quotation from Ben-Gurion, *Test of Fulfillment,* p. 11).

[66] Ben-Gurion, for example, contended that: "The Arabs will acquiesce in Jewish immigration and will accommodate themselves to the new reality when it becomes an established fact" (quoted in *ibid,* p. 12).

undoubtedly real fear of Jewish domination. They believed that this domination would be accomplished were the Jews to realize the principal goals of the Zionist program.[67]

The intervention of the Arab states in Palestine in 1948 was elicited by a number of factors. In the first place, there was a natural reaction against a people who, since their entry into Palestine in relatively significant numbers in the late nineteenth century, had been regarded as foreign interlopers. As the Jewish community grew in numbers and strength, and as it became increasingly conspicuous with the introduction of modern communications into the Middle East, animosity toward the Jews spread to ever-greater numbers of Arabs who, although physically remote, had become aware of the existence and growth in Palestine of a self-consciously alien community.

In the second place there were considerations of power politics. The Arabs as a people and the several Arab states, both individually and collectively, came to fear the Jews. Specifically, the Arabs came to dread that they would fall under Jewish hegemony in view of the superior technical and financial expertise of the Jews, their access to relatively large sums of capital, and their proven ability to enlist the diplomatic and political support of geographically remote but politically proximate great powers.[68]

[67] The distinguished Arab historian, Philip K. Hitti, in his testimony before the Anglo-American Committee of Inquiry, for example, declared that: "Jewish immigration seems to us an attenuated form of conquest" (quoted in Crum, *Silken Curtain,* p. 22).

[68] One Arab politician, intuitively grasping the conventional wisdom of international relations theory, feared that "the Arabs are still weak, and the dangers of Jewish aggression,

The personal rivalry among the rulers of the Arab countries—in particular, the competition between King Farouk and King Abdullah for leadership of the Arab world—played a major role in fostering the deepening involvement of the Arab states in the Palestine struggle. A recurrent theme in the history of international relations—the necessity of competitors for preeminence within a regional international system preventing one another from monopolizing participation in a significant issue, and the possible gains in power, territory, or prestige which might accrue from such a monopoly of participation—has proven an important theme in the history of Middle Eastern international politics since World War II.

In 1947 and 1948, King Abdullah sought, initially by treating with the Jews and later by exploiting his alliance with the British and intervening militarily in Palestine, to make territorial acquisitions there.[69] Egypt and Saudi Arabia wished to avoid becoming involved in a war with the Jews, but nevertheless felt compelled to do so, out of envy of and hostility toward Abdullah and out of fear of his expansionist tendencies.[70] The predatory impulses of Transjordan and Syria (which desired to acquire portions of northern Palestine) led, through the operation of the dynamic of the struggle for power and position among the Arab states, to the entanglement of all of them in the Palestine

---

expansion, and lust for conquest which is likely to develop will inevitably provoke a bloody clash for hegemony over the East" (Taked-Din, a Lebanese diplomat who was a cousin of the Lebanese prime minister, Riadh Bey es-Solh, in a conversation with David Horowitz, quoted in Horowitz, *State in the Making,* p. 100).

[69] Kimche, *Clash of Destinies,* p. 48.
[70] Sharef, *Three Days,* p. 30.

conflict, and to the ultimate fixation of the Middle Eastern international system upon the Palestine question.[71]

The growing force of Arab nationalism also exerted an influence on the Arab states, especially on Egypt. The insecurity of tenure of the Arab elites made them unwilling to defy popular pressure. And once Egypt had intervened in Palestine, its government became a prisoner of its own bombastic propaganda.

All of these factors combined to produce an uncompromising attitude among the Arab states with respect to the Palestine issue. This intransigence was to force the contest with the Jews onto the battlefield, with disastrous consequences for the Arabs.

Arab inflexibility manifested itself in 1946, when the Arab states unequivocally rejected the Report of the Anglo-American Committee of Inquiry, despite the fact that the committee's report recognized that the Arabs of Palestine "rightly look upon Palestine

[71] Systemic considerations dictated Syrian and Saudi intervention in Palestine. For, despite Transjordan's small population, the superiority of its army to the other Arab armies, its intimate relationship with a great power intent upon preserving its own heretofore paramount position in the Middle East, and the superior ability of Transjordan's ruler, suggested the possibility that the considerable accretion to Abdullah's power which would result from his securing control over a large part, if not all, of the most highly developed area within the Arab world might be sufficient to jeopardize the security of the traditional object of his ambition—Syria—and that of his dynastic arch-enemy—Saudi Arabia.

Abdullah's motives for seeking to acquire as much of Palestine as possible were defensive as well as offensive: the Transjordanian monarch feared a powerful Jewish state on the Jordan, or the establishment there of a Palestinian Arab state under the rule of his old enemy, the Mufti of Jerusalem. See Sir John Bagot Glubb, *A Soldier with the Arabs* (London, 1957), p. 63.

as their homeland,"[72] and despite the fact that the report did not express support for the Zionist demand for Jewish statehood.

In refusing to accept the report, the Arabs missed the dual opportunity of embarrassing the Zionists by showing themselves more reasonable than their hated enemy, and of confronting the Zionists with the dilemma of either accepting the report, and thereby binding themselves morally to Anglo-American mediation (with the likely result that Zionist ambitions would be at least partially frustrated), or repecting it, thereby offending the United States and cutting the ground from under the American Zionists.[73]

By maintaining an adamantly unyielding posture toward the demands of the *Yishuv,* the Arab states committed themselves to oppose Zionist aims by force. While Arab violence against the *Yishuv* had yielded short-term gains for the Arabs during the mandatory period,[74] an internal change—the shift of the balance of forces within the Middle East in favor of the Jews—and external developments— the more-or-less complete neutralization of the pro-Arab great power overlord (Britain), and the growing ascendancy in the Middle East of a relatively pro-Zionist great power (the United States)

---

[72] The Anglo-American Committee of Inquiry, *Report to the United States Government and to His Majesty's Government in the United Kingdom* (Washington, 1946), p. 4.

[73] For the division within the Jewish Agency on how to respond to the report, see Horowitz, *State in the Making,* p. 94.

[74] The gains were not long-term. The limited successes of Arab violence during the mandatory period served to convince the *Yishuv* of the need for self-reliance and of the necessity of developing an effective military machine. The consequences of the Arabs' limited successes were thus, in the long-run, disastrous for them.

—suggested that resort to force by the Arabs after World War II would have very different consequences than those it had had prior to that war.

Arab intransigence played a major role in making first partition and then war inevitable. Thus in January 1947, the Arabs refused, at a conference convened by Britain to deal with the Palestine question, to make any concessions. The United Kingdom was hence forced to submit the Palestine question to the U.N. The Zionists benefited greatly from this move: they were able to win the approval of the international organization for their principal objective.[75]

Arab inflexibility also aided the Zionists in that it had a cohesive effect upon the *Yishuv* and led ultimately to a war from which the Jews emerged in possession of considerably more territory than had been allotted to them under the United Nations Partition Plan.

The providential results of Arab obduracy for the Jews were celebrated by the principal Jewish terrorist leader in Palestine, who wrote: "The obstinacy of our enemies rescued us. . . . But for Arab . . . stubbornness, we Jews of Palestine would today be living in a 'Morrison Ghetto'." [76]

The Arab rebuff to UNSCOP deprived the Arabs of the chance of severely circumscribing the territorial extent of the state of Israel. Later, during the Israeli war of independence, Arab irreconcilability again re-

[75] One member of the United Nations Special Committee on Palestine (UNSCOP) has observed how Arab obstinacy damaged the Arab cause: "The Arab Higher Committee's uncompromising attitude, its refusal to consider the possibility of any conciliatory course, was to prove a convincing argument for partition" (quoted in Garcia-Granados, *Birth of Israel*, p. 39).

[76] Begin, *The Revolt*, p. 318.

dounded to the disadvantage of the Arabs. As the expiration date of the first truce of the war approached "It appeared that the Jews were prepared to extend the truce for thirty days." [77] If the Arabs had accepted a prolongation of the truce, during which time the United Nations would undoubtedly have attempted to find a compromise solution, it is quite likely that "a substantial modification of the 1947 partition plan might well have been secured by them." [78] Instead, the Arabs resumed fighting, with calamitous results for them.

In 1948, as in 1967, Arab adamancy played into the hands of the Israeli militants, with the ultimate outcome that because of Israeli military superiority the Arabs lost yet more territory, and the position of the militants within Israel was further strengthened. In the autumn of 1948, as one observer noted: "the Egyptians themselves took a hand in persuading the more hesitant members of the Israeli Government of the need for action in the south." [79] The official Israeli military historian of the war of independence has confirmed this observation that "the Egyptians came to the assistance of the State of Israel. Their obstinate refusal to allow Zahal's convoys free passage into the Negev, contrary to the conditions of the truce, justified military operations against them. Thus the Egyptian army in Palestine dug its own grave." [80]

In view of the balance of military power between the Jews and the Arabs, the Egyptian bombardment of Jewish settlements in the Negev on Octo-

[77] Bernadotte, *Jerusalem*, p. 161.
[78] Glubb, *Soldier with the Arabs*, p. 148.
[79] Kimche, *Clash of Destinies*, p. 240.
[80] Netanel Lorch, *The Edge of the Sword* (New York, 1961), p. 334.

ber 5, 1948, was most unwise. When the Egyptian army, on October 15, 1948, prevented an Israeli convoy from reaching the Jewish settlements in the Negev, it not only violated the truce agreement but it also provided the Israelis with a pretext for launching an offensive against the Egyptian army. This attack was halted on October 22, 1948, when a U.N. cease-fire went into effect. On December 10, 1948, the Egyptians bombarded the Jewish settlement of Nirim in the Negev, and on December 22, they retracted their acceptance of the U.N. armistice resolution, declaring that Egypt would not negotiate until all Israeli troops had withdrawn from the Negev.

The Egyptians thereby repeated their mistake of October 15. On December 22, the Israeli army resumed its offensive against the Egyptian army in the Negev. In this final campaign of the war of independence, Jewish arms were spectacularly successful. The Egyptian army was driven out of the Negev and back across the international boundary into Egypt.

Arab intransigence again proved injurious to Arab interests when the Arabs rejected the Bernadotte Plan, which would have reduced the size of Israel, because the plan recognized the existence of the Jewish state.[81] The Arabs' intractability enabled the Israelis to escape a possible order from the U.N. General Assembly directing them to accept the frontiers Count Bernadotte had proposed, on pain of being subjected to sanctions if they refused.[82]

The Zionists never had any confidence in the United Nations. In particular, they doubted the ability and the willingness of the U.N. to carry out

[81] McDonald, *Mission in Israel,* p. 103.
[82] *Ibid.,* p. 108.

the partition resolution.[83] Their skepticism was to prove well founded in the months that followed.

The Zionists were able to proceed with the establishment of the state of Israel with the sanction of the United Nations because of the assistance rendered them by the United States. The November 29, 1947 Partition Resolution provided the Zionists with an invaluable international imprimatur. It is quite possible that Britain would have provided the Arabs with sufficient assistance to defeat the Jews in 1948 had the U.N. not given its formal approval to the creation of the Jewish state. The partition resolution greatly enhanced Jewish prospects for survival and, at the same time, provided the mandatory power with a face-saving façade with which it could cover its withdrawal from an increasingly intolerable position.[84]

Yet the U.N., in the 1947–48 period, was not much more than an adjunct of American foreign policy. The Zionists recognized that the United Nations was not an independent entity, and this realization contributed to their lack of interest in and respect for it as an institution. As the assistance which the U.N. was able to render Israel declined in later years, reflecting both the reduction of American control over the organization and the tendency

[83] Ben-Gurion, for example, believed that the Jews had to rely upon themselves for protection against the Arabs, despite the Partition Resolution. As Israel's first premier wrote in his reminiscences "What caused me deep anxiety were my doubts about the capacity and willingness of the United Nations to implement its own resolution" (quoted in Ben-Gurion, *Israel, Years of Challenge,* p. 29).

[84] By conferring legitimacy upon the state of Israel, the Partition Resolution also made it easier for first the *Yishuv,* and then Israel, to procure armaments from abroad and diplomatic assistance from the United States at crucial moments. See Safran, *United States and Israel,* p. 39.

of the United States, especially during Republican administrations, to move away from a pro-Israeli posture, Israel's willingness to comply with U.N. resolutions was reduced to the vanishing point.

The Zionists, in the 1945–48 period, had noted the contempt with which the great powers treated the U.N. and the impotence of the international organization. These perceptions, on top of the *Yishuv's* memories of the powerlessness of the League of Nations, confirmed the Zionists in their belief that the international organization could be safely ignored, and should be, save when it was in Israel's interest to heed its pronouncements.

The U.N.'s helplessness with respect to the Palestine question naturally impressed the *Yishuv*. Thus Great Britain, as the Assistant Secretary of the U.N. Palestine Commission observed, did everything in its power to frustrate the commission's work.[85] These subversive efforts were highly successful: as the commission reported to the U.N. General Assembly in April 1948: ". . . lack of cooperation from the Mandatory power" had crippled the work of the commission, in view of the fact that "the Security Council did not furnish the Commission with the necessary armed assistance."[86]

The behavior of the United Nations during the military conflict between the Jews and the Arabs confirmed Zionist estimates of its political feebleness, and reinforced their belief in the indispensability of relying upon Jewish military power and American diplomatic assistance (to neutralize British hostility).

On April 17, 1948, the Security Council appealed

---

[85] Azcarate, *Mission in Palestine,* p. 6.
[86] Quoted in Sharef, *Three Days,* p. 31.

to the Arabs and the Jews to accept a truce. Neither side did so until military necessity compelled them to. On May 6, the General Assembly recommended that a special municipal commission for Jerusalem be appointed. None ever was. On May 14 the General Assembly adopted a resolution authorizing the appointment of a mediator for Palestine. Although a mediator was appointed, he was assassinated and his proposals were rejected in the aftermath of his assassination. Finally, the United Nations failed to threaten to use force, or to actually employ force, in order to halt Arab assaults on the Jews and upon the state which had been established with U.N. sanction. Both the Arabs and the Jews consistently ignored the U.N. in 1948 and 1949, except to call attention to those U.N. resolutions which favored their respective causes. In these respects the two sides established a behavioral pattern which has persisted to the present day.

The Israeli response to U.N. resolutions was determined by Israel's assessment of what action its interests dictated, and of how far it could safely go in disregarding or defying the United Nations.[87] The Israelis had no intention of obeying an organization whose resolutions the Arabs and the great powers flouted whenever it suited them to do so.

One of the most conspicuous features of the Zionist undertaking in Palestine in the 1940s was the successful utilization of force by the Zionists to achieve their objectives. There can be no question

[87] The Israelis, for example, successfully resisted the Truce Commission's attempt to arrange a cease-fire in Jerusalem on May 15, 1948, by preventing Arab delegates from passing through the area under their control to the French Consulate, where the Truce Commission was meeting. See Azcarate, *Mission in Palestine,* pp. 44–45.

that the successful culmination of half a century of Zionist effort owed much to the use of force, both in the form of terrorist tactics in the period preceding the establishment of the state, and in the guise of the traditional military tactics of regular armies during the war of independence.

The terrorist campaign against the British, which was unleashed during the latter part of World War II, was in large measure responsible for compelling the British government to submit the Palestine question to the United Nations. This was both because of the impact it had on British and American public opinion, and because of the effect it had in obliging the predominant Zionist labor movement to adopt a more aggressive policy vis-à-vis Great Britain.[88] The Jews appreciated the utility of terror in their struggle for national independence. They were aware that it was a highly effective technique against an adversary who lacked the will and the ruthlessness to resort to terrorist tactics in retaliation.[89]

The terror was as useful against the Arabs as it was against the British. One sensational terrorist attack, carried out during the civil war which followed the adoption of the U.N. Partition Resolution, was to have a significant impact on a development of the most profound importance in Middle Eastern politics subsequent to the founding of the state of Israel.

On April 9, 1948, *Irgun* and Sternist units cap-

[88] Norman and Helen Bentwich, *Mandate Memories 1918–1948* (New York, 1965), p. 178. British opinion was sickened by the terrorist attacks in Palestine, and clamored for Britain to wash its hands of the place; American opinion, on the other hand, was aroused by the injustices which were being committed against the Jews, and exerted pressure on the American government to work on the Zionists' behalf.

[89] See Begin, *The Revolt,* p. 39.

tured the Arab village of Deir Yassin and massacred more than two hundred men, women, and children. The terrorists' claim that the massacre promoted the Arab exodus from Palestine is well grounded.[90] This mass departure was not only of military significance, but of great political moment as well. As the principal terrorist leader has candidly pointed out in his memoirs: "Of the about 800,000 Arabs who lived on the present territory of the State of Israel, only some 165,000 are still there. The political and economic significance of this development can hardly be overestimated."[91] The refugee issue has, of course, haunted the Middle East down to the present day.

In 1948, as in 1956 and 1967, the Israelis derived enormous benefits from the employment of force. In the 1945–49 period, the Jews were able to compel the British to leave Palestine and to establish effective control over a larger area than had been allocated to them by the United Nations. The utilization of force also profited Israel in that it revealed the disunity and weakness of the Arab states, thus enhancing Israeli morale and emboldening Israeli policy in later years.[92]

The Zionist leaders decided, in accordance with the Herzlian tradition of *Realpolitik* to which they adhered, against specifying the territorial boundaries of the new state, in the hope that Jewish arms would enable the state to acquire more territory than had

[90] For this claim, see Katz, *The Lady*, p. 96.

[91] Begin, *The Revolt*, p. 164.

[92] The Israelis recognized the politico-military frailty of the Arab world at an early date. On July 23, 1948, Ben-Gurion declared: ". . . the military weakness of the Arab states has been exposed. . . . There is also the disclosure of disunity among the Arabs, and their incompetence to stand up to the ordeal" (quoted in Ben-Gurion, *Rebirth and Destiny of Israel*, p. 265).

been assigned to it under the U.N. Partition Resolution.[93]

The Israelis, like most victorious peoples throughout history, desired peace—but peace on their own terms. In arguing that the war "forced upon Israel by Arab aggression"[94] morally invalidated the original partition plan, they sought to disguise their determination to redraw the political map of the Middle East to reflect the altered distribution of power among the states of the region.

The Israelis conformed to the historical norms of successful peoples in another respect as well, as Israeli military success gave rise to expansive tendencies. The Israeli army, having tasted victory in the first phase of the war of independence, was eager for further successes. It opposed accepting the truce of July 18, but was overruled by Ben-Gurion, who acted in response to considerations of overriding political importance.[95] In December 1948, however, the Israeli army defeated the Egyptians in the Negev and then proceeded to cross the international boundary and invade Egypt.

The question of Israel's motivation for invading Sinai in 1948 merits serious attention, as the operative factors have continued to be of great importance in the formulation and execution of Israeli foreign policy, and as the explanation offered by Ben-Gurion has remained the basis of Israel's case for its policies of retaliatory raids, preventive war,

[93] At a meeting of the National Administration on May 12, 1948, the decision to refrain from specifying the boundaries of the new state was taken (Sharef, *Three Days*, p. 132). Ben-Gurion argued frankly that during the forthcoming war the Jews might by force of arms be able to improve the frontiers (Ben-Gurion, *The Jews in Their Land*, p. 331).

[94] Quoted in McDonald, *Mission in Israel*, p. 54.

[95] St. John, *Ben-Gurion*, p. 163.

and, more recently, retention of the Arab territory acquired during the 1967 war.

Certainly, on the tactical military level, the "hot pursuit" factor was at work in December 1948. The Egyptian armed forces, after invading Israel and jeopardizing the existence of the state, had been thrown back across the border, and were being pursued in function of the military dynamic of the situation. But the disciplined military forces of a state which relies for its survival upon the efficacious deployment and performance of its army, and in which supreme authority is vested in a legitimate civilian government, do not cross an international frontier without the express authorization of that government, which in turn directs such action in accordance with its determination of major political and strategic issues. A constellation of factors was probably involved in the Israeli thrust into Sinai: the desire to annihilate physically and psychologically the armed force and that government and people which had posed, and would presumably be able to pose in the future, a serious threat to Israel's security; the hope of compelling Egypt and through her the other Arab states to make peace with Israel, by depriving Egypt of the means to refuse, and by demonstrating Israel's power to make the Arab states pay a heavy price for their opposition; the particular expression of the universal desire of generals and politicians to secure prestige for themselves and glory for their nation; the wish to acquire a buffer zone to protect Israel from future Egyptian attacks; and the normal tendency of new states to test themselves out, to seek self-definition, and to explore the viable outer limits of their power by means of external probes. In a larger sense, the Israeli advance into Sinai and the reluctance with which it was terminated demonstrate Israel's conformity to the near-universal tendency of states to redefine their interests in accordance with the outermost limits of their power.

In the 1945–49 period, the Israelis defined and redefined their essential requirements in a progressively expansive manner. Thus, while the bulk of the *Yishuv* in 1945 would probably have been content with a continuation of the mandate, provided that there was unlimited immigration to Palestine and no restrictions on land purchases, by 1947 a Jewish state with the boundaries the U.N. approved on November 29, 1947, containing an Arab population comprising no more than 45 percent of the total, was the least the Jews would have accepted. A year later, a state one-third larger than that envisioned by the U.N., with an Arab population comprising 10 percent of the whole, was the least favorable solution the *Yishuv* would have consented to. (Finally, in 1949, Israel's threatened expansion into Sinai was halted only because of pressure exerted by outside great powers.)[96]

Israeli foreign policy decisionmakers appreciated, during the independence period, that Israel's freedom of action was limited whenever a determined great power antagonist, which was not neutralized by another great power, acted to prevent the realization of Israeli aspirations. This state of affairs was to persist in future years, with the United States replacing Britain as the power possessing the means and the determination (during the Dulles period, for example) to limit Israel's liberty of movement.

In bowing to the demands of a hostile Great

---

[96] Terence Prittie, *Israel, Miracle in the Desert* (New York, 1967), p. 188.

Britain in January 1949, Ben-Gurion displayed his understanding of the limits on Israel's freedom of action. Great power intervention in 1949 prevented Israel from translating its potential politico-military supremacy in the Middle East into reality, and it was to do so again in the future. The natural course of the evolution of the Middle Eastern international system—the establishment of an Israeli hegemony —has been precluded on three occasions by great power intervention.[97]

Israel, in the independence period, profited from the structure of the developing cold war. Thus the Jewish state was able to secure vital Soviet aid (in the form both of diplomatic support at the United Nations and diplomatic recognition, and, more importantly, in the shape of vitally needed Czech arms at a crucial moment in the military struggle against the Arabs), as British opposition to Israel cast Israel into the role of adversary of the anti-Soviet great power which was at that time preponderant in the Middle East.[98] Simultaneously, Israel was able to retain American support, thanks to the good offices of the American Jewish community. This happy situation was not to recur. After Britain dropped out of the picture, leaving the United States and the Soviet Union as the prin-

[97] In 1948, 1956, and 1967—by Britain, the United States, and the Soviet Union, respectively.

[98] Soviet disappointment with the Arab national movement, which during the 1930s and early 1940s had been pro-German rather than pro-Soviet, and the belief that the Arab states were pro-British whereas the Zionists were fighting Britain contributed to the Soviet decision to support partition (see Walter Z. Laquer, *The Soviet Union and the Middle East* [New York, 1959], p. 146).

The Soviets hoped to eliminate Britain from the Middle East and also to sow discord between the United States and Britain (see Hurewitz, *Struggle,* p. 305).

cipal great power antagonists in the Middle East, Israel was forced to opt for the United States (in view of the Soviets adoption of an unyieldingly anti-Israeli and pro-Arab policy). With nowhere else to turn, dependent on the United States, Israel was subject to intense American pressure whenever the United States found it in its interest to apply such pressure (and whenever domestic political conditions allowed it to do so).

The foreign policy decisionmakers of the state of Israel have been influenced by both the historical experiences of the Jewish people in modern times and by the traditions of Zionist statecraft. These historical experiences have confirmed Israeli diplomacy in the pattern of political realism established by the Zionist movement prior to the foundation of the state.

Israeli foreign policy has been pervaded by the conviction that Israel can realize its vital territorial and political objectives only by means of the successful application of force in its international relations. In conformity with this belief, the state of Israel has sought to insure its security by means of the traditional devices of armaments and alliances. Israeli statesmen, in accordance with their understanding of the power political basis of international politics, have tended to discount the argument that Israel cannot assure its fundamental interests without peacefully reaching a mutually satisfactory settlement with the Arabs.[1]

The roots of Israeli foreign policy extend back to the early days of the modern Zionist movement. In particular, reliance upon force and diplomatic alignment to deal with Middle Eastern opposition to the Israeli program is one fundamental facet of Israeli foreign policy which has its origins in this early period. In the late nineteenth century Herzl

---

* This chapter appeared as an article in substantially the same form in *World Affairs* (Washington, D.C.: American Peace Society), vol. 135 (Summer 1972), and is included here with the permission of the American Peace Society.

[1] For the view that Israeli security can only be insured by an agreement with the Arabs, see Uri Avnery, *Israel without Zionists* (New York, 1968), p. 75.

proposed coping with Turkish and Arab opposition to the development of a Jewish community in Palestine by forging an alliance between the Zionist movement and a European great power.[2] The Zionist movement during the mandatory period followed in Herzl's footsteps. Zionist leaders in the 1920s and 1930s insisted that Arab opposition to the growth of the National Home should be discouraged by a stern and uncompromising attitude on the part of the mandatory power toward Arab disturbers of the peace, rather than by concessions to the Arabs.[3] Those few Jews who advocated binationalism as a solution to the problem of Arab opposition were regarded as traitors to the national cause.[4] Once it became apparent that Britain would not act to effectively contain Arab opposition, the Zionist leadership advocated a policy of relying upon the United States for diplomatic support while directly confronting the Arabs. This remains the policy of Israel today.

Israeli statesmen, in formulating their nation's foreign policy, have been profoundly influenced by a ubiquitous sense of Israel's insecurity.[5] This feeling of insecurity derives from two specific historical sources: the persistent assaults by the Arabs against

[2] See Theodor Herzl, *The Complete Diaries of Theodor Herzl* (New York and London, 1960), II: 566, 655 ff.; and IV:1578–79. Also, see Theodor Herzl, *The Jewish State* (New York, 1946), p. 76.

[3] See Ben-Gurion, *The Jews in Their Land* (London, 1966), p. 300; Meinertzhagen, *Middle East Diary* (London, 1959), pp. 141–42; Kisch, *Palestine Diary* (London, 1938), p. 184; Bentwich, *Mandate Memories 1918–1948* (New York, 1965), p. 161.

[4] Bentwich, *Mandate Memories,* p. 119.

[5] For one leading Israeli statesman's perception of this insecurity, see Moshe Dayan, "Israel's Border and Security Problems," *Foreign Affairs* 33 (January 1955): 252–53.

the *Yishuv* and then the state of Israel and the Nazi holocaust. While the failure of the British guarantor to fulfill its protective function during the mandatory period led to the disillusionment of Zionist leaders with regard to the security of the *Yishuv's* position and the reliability of great power benefactors, the failure of the great powers to impede the progress of the Nazi murder machine destroyed forever any lingering hopes that the Jews could expect great power assistance at critical moments.

Israeli decisionmakers' perception of the Arabs as an implacably hostile force similarly originates in the memory of what has in fact been a long history of Arab antagonism toward the Jews in Palestine.[6] Indeed, Israeli policymakers continue to believe that the Arabs are committed to the annihilation of Israel.[7]

Israeli statesmen, although acutely aware of the intense hostility of the Arab states toward Israel and of the danger this animosity creates, have failed to consider Arab enmity in the light of Arab grievances. In refusing to recognize that the very existence of a relatively powerful, westernized state in the midst of the Arab world must inevitably focus the attention and animosity of the Arab nations upon a potentially dangerous (because powerful) state, Israel has persisted in the Zionist tradition of denying that there is any understandable, not to mention objectively valid, basis for Arab apprehen-

[6] For a statement by a prominent Israeli statesman that the Arabs will neither live in peace with Israel nor permit Israel to live in peace, see Abba Eban, *The Security Situation in the Middle East* (New York, 1953), p. 9.

[7] See Golda Meir, *This Is Our Strength: Selected Papers of Golda Meir* (New York, 1962), ed. by Henry M. Christman, p. 78. This conviction has, needless to say, intensified Israel's proclivity to rely upon force in its dealings with the Arabs.

sion and hostility toward Israel. This denial is attributable in part to the universal tendency of states to justify their behavior by denying that their antagonists possess legitimate grievances, and in part to the introversion of Israeli nationalism.

Indeed, the self-absorption of this nationalism has served, by preserving Israeli unawareness of the source of Arab anxiety, to insulate the Israelis from qualms which might have interfered with Israel's forceful pursuit of its own interest. The Israelis' ability to enjoy a clear conscience has enabled them to refuse to satisfy those Arab claims the satisfaction of which would undermine the viability of the state of Israel. In particular, the necessity of repatriating or compensating Arab refugees—a costly, and perhaps disastrous, operation—has been obviated.[8]

Israel's reluctance to make substantial concessions to the Arabs has been engendered by an historically conditioned determination to avoid the disastrous consequences of appeasement, and by the conviction that the Arabs are too weak, in any event, to interfere with Israeli plans. Indeed, the Zionists have, since Herzl's time, tended to regard the Arabs as being incapable of thwarting Zionist aspirations in

[8] The exodus of the Palestinian Arabs during the 1948 war was of immense economic benefit to the state of Israel, which was in dire economic straits at the time of its establishment. The abandoned refugee property, which Israel appropriated for the settlement of Jewish immigrants (whose presence was urgently required for security reasons) was estimated by the Palestine Conciliation Commission to have been worth more than $600 million. The Conciliation Commission estimated that 80 percent of Israel's total acreage consisted of land which had been abandoned by the Arab refugees. For details regarding the economic importance to the state of Israel of the refugee departure, see Don Peretz, *Israel and the Palestine Arabs* (Washington, 1958), pp. 143, 186.

Palestine. This initial Zionist evaluation of the political impotence of the Arabs has been confirmed by the evident inability of the Arabs to halt the growth of the National Home during the period of the British mandate, and by the Arab defeats of 1948, 1956, and 1967.

Israeli diplomacy has been built around the attempt to secure the sponsorship, protection, and assistance of the most powerful state within the international system—the United States. In this respect, it displays a basic continuity with Zionist statecraft which, from its inception, sought to enlist one or another of the great powers—preferably the most potent—to act as patron of the Zionist enterprise. The nature of the Israeli appeal for great power sponsorship similarly continues in the tradition established by Zionist statecraft. Thus, as the Zionists under Herzl and Weizmann claimed that the existence of a strong Jewish community in Palestine would serve to promote the political interest of the Jews' great power benefactor, Israel has contended that its existence and prosperity benefits its patron, as Israel is able to perform regional order-maintaining tasks which its protector would find it inconvenient, and possibly highly dangerous, to undertake directly.

Herzl and Weizmann stressed the strategic significance of Palestine, which guards the eastern flank of the Suez Canal, and could serve as a regional source of influence for its sponsor. Similarly, Israeli leaders have suggested that the United States, through an Israeli surrogate, can retain a certain measure of control over political and territorial developments in the Middle East, and can at the same time block the growth of Soviet influence in the region. Specifically, it is the threat of Israeli military intervention which precludes the absorption of Jordan by more powerful Arab states, and which presumably deters overt Communist take-overs in several Arab nations.[9]

The state of Israel, like the Zionist movement before it, has been guided in its selection of a great power patron by considerations of power and availability rather than by moral criteria. Thus Israel has sought to secure the United States as its guardian in view of America's puissance and the size and influence of the American Jewish community, the hostility of the Soviet Union, the weakness of France, and the pro-Arab orientation of British policymakers, in the same way as Herzl and Weizmann, in light of the antagonistic attitude of the Ottoman and Russian empires, the unresponsiveness of Germany, the unreliability of France, and the unavailability of the United States, sought to enroll Great Britain as sponsor of the Zionist program.

Dependence upon a geographically remote great power benefactor has remained a salient feature of Israeli foreign policy since the founding of the state. Diplomatically, Israel continues to rely upon American support against possible massive Soviet military intervention in the Middle East, much as she depended upon American diplomatic assistance to offset British enmity and to preclude decisive British military intervention against her in the period following World War II. Economically, the Jewish

[9] It appears that Israel's policy of providing economic assistance to a number of sub-Saharan African states is motivated in part by the desire to demonstrate to the United States Israel's serviceability as a vehicle for containing the growth of Communist influence within selected areas of the underdeveloped world. See Nadav Safran, *The United States and Israel* (Cambridge, 1963), p. 267.

state continues to rely upon contributions from American Jews. Finally, in the military sphere, Israel continues to depend upon the United States for the provision of sophisticated military aircraft.[10]

Israel's need to rely upon its great power patron when fundamental Israeli interests are at stake is extremely distasteful to the Israelis, not only because of the natural desire of states to retain freedom of action at critical moments, nor solely because dependence upon others is a contradiction of the basic Zionist tenet of self-reliance, but also because of Israel's memory of the historical unreliability of great powers in moments of supreme crisis for the *Yishuv* and the state of Israel in the past. The Chamberlain White Paper is not forgotten, nor is the failure of the western powers to attempt to disrupt the Nazi slaughter machine. Similarly, America's failure to prevent Egypt from acquiring dangerously large quantities of Czech arms in 1955, to offset this accretion to Egyptian power by providing Israel with equivalent military equipment or a se-

[10] The United States rendered crucially important diplomatic assistance to Israel in 1946, when American pressure led to the appointment of the Anglo-American Committee of Inquiry, in 1947, when the United States procured the necessary votes to secure passage of the United Nations Partition Resolution, and in 1948, when the United States extended prompt recognition to the state of Israel. American economic assistance was inaugurated in 1949 when the American-dominated Export-Import Bank granted a $100 million loan to Israel. In the critical years between 1948 and 1955 Israel received $1 billion in aid from the U.S. Government and American Jewry. This aid enabled Israel to absorb 800,000 immigrants and to develop the economic infrastructure of the country. Plagued by popular insistence upon the maintenance of a high standard of living and lacking an adequate resource base, Israel remains dependent upon economic assistance from the United States and from the American Jewish community to finance her economic development.

curity guarantee, to permit Israel to retain the Sinai buffer after the 1956 war, or to compel the Egyptians to disperse their troop concentrations in Sinai in 1967 has impressed the Israelis with the idea that reliance upon their great power protector is dangerous and has encouraged a tendency to take preventive action.

The *Yishuv's* experience of seeing Britain detach herself from the Zionist embrace in order to win Arab good will and prevent Britain's great power adversary—Germany—from gaining influence in the Middle East, conditioned Israel to expect the United States to pursue a similar course of action. Yet, despite this pessimistic expectation, Israeli policymakers understood that Israel was inevitably dependent upon a measure of great power support.[11] Israeli statesmen were thus confronted with a serious dilemma.

Israeli policymakers sought a way out of this dilemma in the following manner: while Israel's great power benefactor had on critical occasions failed to render the Jewish state positive support, neither the protector nor the United Nations had prevented Israel from using force on its own behalf. Israel in 1948, 1956, and 1967 had been able to utilize force with decisive effect. The realization that Israel could use force successfully inclined Israeli decisionmakers to resort to force whenever fundamental Israeli interests appeared to be jeopardized.

---

[11] Israeli statesmen acknowledged this dependence at the beginning of Israeli history. Thus the Israeli diplomat, David Horowitz, noted in his memoirs that American assistance was indispensable in securing the adoption of the U.N. Partition Resolution. Horowitz believed that the state of Israel would not have come into existence without the resolution. See Horowitz, *State in the Making* (New York, 1953), p. 306.

Since the founding of the state, Israeli political leaders have been engaged in an ongoing debate over the proper course for Israeli foreign policy to pursue. This foreign policy debate, which has its origins in the struggle between the moderates and the activists during the mandatory period, has always revolved around three issues: the advisability, or necessity, of utilizing force to attain the principal Zionist objectives; the merits of self-reliance, as opposed to dependence upon a great power patron; and the possibility of peacefully reaching a mutually satisfactory agreement with the Arabs. The militants, both in the pre-state era and in the period since the establishment of the state, have tended to argue that the achievement of Zionist aims requires the employment of force. The activists have stressed the necessity for self-reliance, the undependability of the great powers, and the futility of attempting to reach a settlement with the Arabs. The moderates, on the other hand, have tended to disagree with the activists on each of these points.

Between 1948 and 1963, David Ben-Gurion led the militant faction within the Israel government. Ben-Gurion has emphasized the necessity of using force, arguing in particular that only by pursuing a tough policy of reprisals could Israel expect to deter future Arab attacks.[12] Ben-Gurion and his adherents have always been suspicious of the intentions of the great powers. They have believed that only by demonstrating the will and determination to survive could Israel win the friendship of these powers.[13] Militants outside of the government have taken a

[12] See Naphtali Lau-Lavie, *Moshe Dayan* (London, 1968), p. 118.

[13] Maurice Edelman, *Ben-Gurion: A Political Biography* (London, 1964), p. 169.

more extreme position: they have contended that a policy of territorial expansion would bolster Israel's security position by creating a buffer zone between Israel and the Arab states.[14]

The moderates, led for most of Israeli history by Moshe Sharett, have advocated a policy of co-operation with the Western great powers, rather than a policy of retaliatory raids, to deter *fedayeen* attacks. In the period prior to the 1956 war Sharett and his associates hoped to procure a security guarantee from the Western great powers. They were also optimistic about the possibility of establishing direct contact with the Arab governments.[15]

The pacifistically-inclined *Mapam* went beyond Sharett's essentially prudential argument against the retaliatory policy and the policy of preventive war, insisting that preventive war would constitute an unacceptable violation of ethical principles.[16]

The militants won the 1955–56 debate, as they had won the 1948 debate. In the crisis which culminated in the 1967 war, another foreign policy decision of overriding importance was taken by the Israeli government against the background of the militant-moderate debate. The activists, summoning their usual array of arguments, warned that the Arabs would accelerate their demands if Israel accepted the Egyptian blockade of the Gulf of

[14] For excerpts from a speech to this effect by Ya'qov Meridor, a member of the *Knesset* belonging to the *Herut* party, see Ernest Stock, *Israel on the Road to Sinai* (Ithaca, 1967), p. 162.

[15] Lau-Lavie, *Moshe Dayan*, p. 107.

[16] For excerpts from a speech to this effect by Ya'qov Hazan, a member of the *Knesset* belonging to the *Mapam* party, see Stock, *The Road to Sinai*, pp. 157–58.

Aqaba.[17] They were skeptical about the possibility that the United States would act to protect Israeli interests.[18] The Israeli public, sharing the militants' skepticism about the dependability of external aid, pressed the government to take a firm stand against Nasser. As in 1948 and 1956, the militants prevailed.

The historical memory of the Jewish people has played a major role in the shaping of Israeli foreign policy. Israel's disinclination to make any major concessions to the Arabs, as well as its adoption of the policy of retaliatory raids, was significantly influenced by the Jews' memory of the catastrophic consequences which ultimately resulted from the West's appeasement of Hitler in the 1930s.

The Israeli government's decision to institute a policy of reprisal raids was influenced by another set of historical memories as well. The *Yishuv* had been able, by resorting to armed self-defense, to limit Jewish casualties in the face of Arab attacks in 1929 and in the 1936–39 period. Several years later the *Irgun* and the Stern Group had successfully utilized force in their terror policy against first, the mandatory power, and then, the Palestinian Arabs. These memories strengthened the resolve to meet force with force.

The Israeli tendency to take Arab threats of extermination at face value similarly derived from the Jews' memory of the persistent enmity of the Arabs toward the *Yishuv* during the twentieth century, of the succession of Arab attacks during the mandatory

[17] Walter Z. Laqueur, *The Road to War, 1967* (London, 1968), p. 95 (hereafter cited as *War*).
[18] Theodore Draper, *Israel and World Politics* (New York, 1968), p. 24.

117

period, and of the Nazi attempt to annihilate European Jewry.

Israel in 1955 thus put the most pessimistic possible construction upon Nasser's acquisition of Czech arms: Egypt had purchased these weapons solely to destroy Israel. The Israelis did not consider that other factors—such as Nasser's desire to impress his people, to placate the Egyptian military, upon whose continued support his political survival was contingent, or to further Egyptian ambitions in other parts of the Arab world—might have motivated him to conclude the agreement with Czechoslovakia. Israel's interpretation of Egyptian intentions in the crisis of May 1967, similarly, and with equally good reason, assumed the worst.

Israeli foreign policy from the very first has been formulated without reference to the wishes of the United Nations, except in those instances when the United States has strongly supported the U.N. position. Israel's disregard of the United Nations sprang from the Jewish state's perception of the impotence of that organization. Israel's attitude toward the United Nations had its roots in the period of the British mandate. The U.N.'s predecessor—the League of Nations—revealed, during the period of its existence, a total inability to prevent Britain from abridging in the White Papers of 1922, 1930, and 1939 what the Jews considered to be their internationally recognized rights in Palestine. The League's successor demonstrated similar powerlessness, from Israel's viewpoint, at crucial moments subsequent to the founding of the state. Thus the United Nations failed to provide Israel with military assistance in 1948 when Arab armies attacked in violation of United Nations resolutions. In the years following the establishment of the state, the U.N. failed to compel Egypt to comply with the resolution calling upon her to open the Suez Canal to the passage of Israeli ships. The United Nations was unable, in 1955, to prevent the consummation of the intensely destabilizing Czech-Egyptian arms deal, and was either unwilling or unable to offer Israel a means of offsetting the advantages Egypt thereby acquired. Finally, by yielding to Egyptian demands for the withdrawal of the United Nations Emergency Force from Sinai in the spring of 1967 without first consulting Israel, the United Nations allowed Israel's security to be placed in grave jeopardy.

These repeated U.N. failures confirmed the Israeli predilection for being guided by the *Realpolitik* tradition of Zionist statecraft. This tradition stressed the indispensability of self-help at crucial moments, in view of the proven unreliability of external forces.

The Israeli belief that the survival of the state is contingent upon Israeli military superiority over the Arabs and upon the willingness to utilize this superiority has decisively influenced Israeli foreign policy. In view of the impossibility of relying upon the assistance of either the great powers or the United Nations, and in view of the historical success of the policy of military self-reliance—as in the Arab rebellion of 1936–39, and the wars of 1948, 1956, and 1967—Israel has tended to conceive of the alternatives confronting it at critical moments as being either preventive military action or destruction at the hands of the Arab states, and has thus been inclined to opt for preventive war.[19]

Domestic political considerations have tradition-

[19] In 1956, for example, Israeli leaders believed that Israel had only two options: preventive war or annihilation. For a statement of this view, see Meir, *This Is Our Strength,* p. 78.

119

ally disposed the Israel government to adopt a militant foreign policy. Specifically, the existence of a powerful political party which has always advocated an activist foreign policy, and the strong tendency of the Israeli public in general to favor a very tough position whenever the security of the state appears to be threatened, have led the ruling party within Israel to adopt a considerably more combative foreign policy than might otherwise have been the case.

This tendency has been apparent since the days of World War II, when the Labor Zionist leaders shifted to a tougher line toward the British, largely in order to counter the growing popularity which the *Irgun* enjoyed within the *Yishuv* as a consequence of its aggressively anti-British policy.

The policy of retaliation which Israel adopted after the war of independence represented an extension of the traditional Zionist policy of self-defense. The state of Israel, because of the persisting Arab refusal to permit it to pursue peacefully its program of internal development, carried the military conflict to Arab territory. It was able to do this thanks to both the superiority of Israeli striking power and the absence of a great power possessed of both the will and the ability to inhibit the Israeli response. In these respects, it was more fortunate than the *Yishuv* had been.

Pressure for the rigorous application of the policy of reprisals came from the Israeli public, which made its wishes clear in the *Knesset* elections of July 1, 1955. (In these elections, the militant *Herut* and *Ahdut ha-Avodah* parties scored sizable gains). The government, alarmed by the growing popularity of the militants, and fearful of a continuation of the trend, was prodded into adopting a harsher policy

120

toward Egypt. Ben-Gurion returned to power, and Sharett's moderate policy was set aside.[20]

As the pressure of public opinion played a significant role in leading the Israeli government to adopt the policy of preventive war in 1956, it similarly pushed the Eshkol government into adopting a more bellicose stance. The danger of being outflanked by more militant politicians deterred Premier Eshkol (who was hopeful that Egypt would eventually come to terms with Israel) from responding to Tunisian President Bourguiba's 1963 peace feelers.[21] This same fear led the Eshkol government, following the recrudescence of commando attacks in 1965, to institute a tough retaliatory policy.

The same behavioral pattern was evident in the wake of the 1967 war, when the government was committed to forward positions as a consequence of public statements made by Defense Minister Moshe Dayan to the effect that Israel would not withdraw from Jerusalem, the Gaza Strip, or the West Bank. The realities of domestic politics precluded the possibility that the government could repudiate either Dayan or his statements.

The tendency of Israeli statesmen to rely upon force, and the threat of force, as the central components of their policy toward the Arab states has

[20] For the view that the Israeli public feared that intolerable damage to Israel's security position would result from the Czech-Egyptian arms deal unless remedial action were taken, see Earl Berger, *The Covenant and the Sword: Arab-Israeli Relations, 1948–56* (London, 1965), p. 207. For the view that the Israeli public, in the 1965–67 period, pressed for the adoption of a vigorous retaliatory policy out of the fear that failure to do so would lead to an intensification of *Fatah* attacks, see Laqueur, *War,* p. 47.

[21] See Aubrey Hodes, *Dialogue With Ishmael: Israel's Future in the Middle East* (New York, 1968), p. 76.

been strongly influenced by Israeli confidence that the clash of arms is likely to culminate in a favorable outcome for Israel. This assurance has been instilled by the long series of Jewish military successes against the Arabs—victories which began in 1929, when the Jews in the collective settlements successfully resisted Arab attacks.

Israel has derived significant benefits from the employment of force. Thus Israel's triumph in the 1948 war brought her control over a portion of Palestine; her victory in the 1956 war produced the annihilation of the Egyptian army, which had been developing into a serious menace, the destruction of Egypt's will to fight, and the acquisition of another decade in which to augment the power of the Jewish state. Israel's triumph in the 1967 war brought her significant territorial gains.[22] That Israel could reasonably expect both to be successful in a military conflict with the Arabs and to enjoy substantial advantages as a result of military victory could not fail to make armed conflict, at the very least, not entirely unpalatable to Israeli decisionmakers and to the Israeli public.

Israel has, since the 1967 war, demonstrated certain expansionist propensities. While Israel's obvious disinclination to abandon the territories it conquered in that war stems in part from the belief (reasonable in view of the persisting animosity of the Arab states and the proven unreliability of the great powers and the United Nations) that the territorial

[22] For statements by Israeli leaders regarding the improvement in Israel's security position which resulted from the 1967 war, see Ben-Gurion, *Israel: Years of Challenge,* pp. 132–60; Abba Eban, quoted in Anthony Moncrieff, editor, *Suez: Ten Years After* (New York, 1966), p. 75; and Moshe Dayan, *Diary of the Sinai Campaign* (London, 1966), p. 206.

security of the state can be insured only by retaining control over adjacent territories, it also derives to some extent from an immanent tendency to expand. This expansive proclivity is not unique to Israel, but appears to be common to all states, with the possible exception of those which, having experienced crushing defeats in past ages, and having reorganized their national existence along satisfactory, albeit essentially nonpower political lines, have successfully sublimated the desire to expand territorially.[23]

The Zionist movement, since its founding by Herzl, has possessed an expansive tendency in the sense that it sought from the first to acquire territory which it did not initially possess. This bias is attributable to a combination of factors: the perennial disposition of states to define their interests in proportion to the potential for expansion afforded by the distribution of power within the international system of which they are a part; a rational assessment that the security of Israel can be assured only by occupying additional territories; the desire to acquire Arab territory for use as a bargaining counter in future political negotiations with the Arabs; a desire to restore Israel to the territorial dimensions it enjoyed in biblical times; the sheer forward momentum of a state in motion; and domestic political considerations.

The first significant penetration of Egyptian territory by Israeli military forces took place in December 1948, when Israeli army units invaded Sinai. The second noteworthy penetration occurred

[23] Sweden would be an example of such a power. States which live under the shadow of an overwhelmingly powerful nation seem to be immune to such expansive propensities; they apparently recognize the futility with which efforts at expansion are likely to be crowned.

in October 1956 when the Israeli army attacked and occupied the entire Sinai Peninsula. In both instances Israel withdrew its armed forces with great reluctance in the face of intense diplomatic pressure. The two incidents bespeak an Israeli inclination to seek to occupy and hold Egyptian territory. The third significant Israeli military incursion into Arab territory took place during the 1967 war when the Israeli army invaded and occupied the Sinai Peninsula, the West Bank, the Golan Heights, and Jerusalem. Thanks to a favorable constellation of diplomatic forces, Israel has been able to keep possession of the territories it conquered in the course of the war.

In the period following the 1967 war, the Israeli government, by declining to accept a return to the 1949 armistice frontiers, acted precisely as it had in the wake of the war of independence, when it refused to accept a reversion to the boundaries specified by the 1947 U.N. Partition Resolution. In both cases, Israel displayed a tendency to acquire and retain as much Arab territory as possible.

Since its creation by Herzl, political Zionism has subordinated all considerations to the primary objective of creating the state of Israel. Israeli statecraft, drawing its inspiration from this source, has valued the maintenance of the territorial integrity of the state of Israel above everything else. The consequences of this value system have been the adoption of a firm policy toward the Arabs and the rejection of such concessions as refugee repatriation or compensation, which could reduce Arab grievances and thus conceivably result in the reduction of tension between Israel and the Arab states.

V. ISRAELI IMPERIALISM: FROM SECURITY TO SETTLEMENT

Israel's expansionist policy springs from the imperative security requirements of a geographically vulnerable state whose existence is perpetually jeopardized by the apparently irremediable hostility of the states which surround her on three sides. The two outstanding features of Israeli psychology—a very deeply rooted sense of insecurity, which is based upon a long series of historical experiences, and a profound mistrust of great powers, the rationality of which has been confirmed again and again by the experiences of the Zionist movement, the *Yishuv,* and the state of Israel over the past eight decades— foreordain the adoption of an imperialistic policy by the state of Israel in light of the refusal of the Arab states to come to terms.

The rationality of an expansionist policy in these circumstances appears to the Israelis to be incontestable in view of the persistent unwillingness of the Arabs to reach a settlement, the obvious historical failure of alternative policies of conciliation, retaliation, and preventive war, and the conventional proclivity of states to appreciate the advantages a successful forward policy can be expected to confer: the acquisition of strategic territories for utilization as buffers and bargaining counters, the deterrence of future aggressive acts by the enemy, and the demoralization of the war party, followed by the accession to power of the peace party within the enemy state.

In addition to these external factors, internal considerations are of considerable importance in leading Israel to adopt an imperialistic policy. The most significant domestic determinant of Israeli foreign policy is the existence within Israel of a powerful "party of movement." This party, *Herut* (now part of *Gahal*), has for more than two decades exercised substantial influence over Israeli foreign policy. *Herut* has been able to exert pressure from the Right because of the widespread popularity of its aggressive foreign policy position with the Israeli electorate. The need to protect itself from being outflanked on the crucial foreign policy issue has compelled the dominant *Mapai* (now the most important component of the Israel Labor party) to pursue a foreign policy course which has, given the obstinacy of Arab opposition, found its logical culmination in an expansionist policy. A second important domestic source of Israeli imperialism has been the existence of serious tensions between the two principal segments of the Israeli population —the Ashkenazic and the Sephardic Jews. States riven by domestic social, economic, or ethnic conflict are prone to adopt an aggressive foreign policy. Such a course constitutes a relatively easy and painless method of dealing with serious internal strains. It is far less painful than doing nothing, thereby allowing animosities to become exacerbated to the point where the social fabric is seriously damaged, and far easier than either inducing or compelling the privileged classes and groups within society to surrender their privileges for the sake of the common good. Israel's expansionist policy has in part been motivated by the desire to relieve the ethnic problem in Israel.

Israeli foreign policy has limited goals. The state of Israel has not embarked upon a full-blown expansionist policy, nor has it developed a thoroughgoing imperialist mentality. Such a mentality— which is characterized by the conviction that the

security of the state and the integrity of the fundamental institutions of the state are contingent upon
the security of the empire which the state possesses;
the security of the imperial possessions in turn neces-
sitating, as a rule, further expansion—has not taken
root in Israel. This mentality has not developed
partly as a consequence of the traditional introversion of Zionism (which, though modified by the
persistence of the external threat, has not been entirely supplanted), partly as a result of the lingering inhibitory influence of the ethical precepts of socialism, and partly because Israel was not able,
until 1967, to acquire and retain an empire, the indispensable prerequisite for the evolution of a comprehensive imperialistic outlook.

The modified imperialist viewpoint which Israel
has developed and which it is unlikely to abandon
has important policy implications. The state of
Israel is committed to the preservation of Israeli
security by means of the retention of certain strategic
positions, notably Sharm el-Sheikh, the Golan
Heights, the West Bank, and the Gaza Strip.
Israel is also committed to maintaining a favorable
overall military balance vis-à-vis the Arab states.
This does not necessarily require an absolute quanti-
tative superiority over the combined strength of the
principal Arab states in all categories of weapons
and military forces, in view of the unquestionable
qualitative superiority of the Israeli armed forces
and the lack of unity and coordination among the
military forces of the Arab states. It does, however,
require overall Israeli superiority in the air arm and
in missiles.

Israeli policy, as another of its irreducible objectives, requires preventing any Arab state from acquiring nuclear weapons. Another major aim of

Israeli policy is to preclude the unification of the principal Arab states under the hegemony of any of their number except under such conditions as Israel may find it in its interest to sanction. Israeli policy is predicated upon the assumption that Israeli security rests, and will for the foreseeable future continue to rest, upon the maintenance of a favorable distribution of power between Israel and the Arab states. Conventional balance of power considerations thus require preventive action by Israel whenever necessary to forestall developments within any of the Arab states which are likely to result in a significant increase in Arab military power as a whole.

Israeli policy, in summary, seeks the maintenance of a favorable military balance between Israel and the Arab states, physical control over certain vital strategic points, and the preclusion of Arab unification, in order to preserve the security of the state.

Israeli foreign policy is not essentially annexationist. Pragmatic considerations counsel strongly against such a course. In addition, there are ethical objections, strong fears about the corrosive impact of an annexationist policy upon the democratic institutions of the state, and the risks of superpower intervention. Israeli foreign policy does not seek economic dominion over the Middle East, nor does it seek leadership of the region as an end per se.

Nevertheless, it is inconceivable that Israel would, in view of her past experiences with great powers, be satisfied by any American security guarantee, however apparently watertight. A consideration of the psychology of the Israeli people and of the experiences which have molded that psychology must lead to the conclusion that Israel will not accept any settlement with the Arab states which fails to fulfill her unalterable minimum requirements.

Middle Eastern international politics has, since 1948, been dominated by two parallel conflicts: the Arab-Israeli struggle and the opposition of various Arab states to the Egyptian drive for paramountcy within the Arab world.

The Egyptian drive for primacy can be said to have begun in 1945 with the formation of the Arab League. Subsequent to the overthrow of the monarchy in 1952 and the emergence of Nasser in 1954 as the ruler of Egypt, Egypt resumed her bid for hegemony. Nasser sought to attain a two-fold position for Egypt: unchallenged ascendancy in the Arab world, and the status of a significant actor in world politics as leader of the Arab bloc. Of prime importance to Egypt was blocking the unification of Syria and Iraq, unless those two states were unified under Egyptian auspices. The creation of a united state occupying the entire Fertile Crescent, unless accomplished under Egyptian sponsorship and control, would raise an Arab power strong enough to thwart Egypt's hegemonic ambitions.

The goals of Egyptian foreign policy were more intangible than those of Israeli foreign policy. Egyptian imperialism was (and remains) cultural and psychological in nature, without any specific territorial basis. Egypt sought to achieve a position which would make it arbiter of the Arab world. In this role, Egyptian sanction would be required for all significant political changes within and among the Arab states. The foreign and domestic policies of the other Arab states would be brought into conformity with those of Egypt. The Arab world as a whole would look to Egypt in all matters of importance for leadership and inspiration.

Although Egypt did not seek physical control over other Arab states, her claim to universal Arab deference compelled her to strive for the establishment of a dependable client regime in Syria in order to preclude the creation of a hostile Iraqi-Syrian union. Nasser was thus constrained to seek supreme political power for his adherents in Syria. In addition, in order to make good Egypt's claim to be the legitimate arbiter of the Arab world, Nasser was compelled to take military action in Yemen and to risk war with Iraq over Kuwait in 1961. Egypt attempted to realize her quest for dominance in the Arab world by acquiring sole title to the three movements of anti-imperialism, Arab unity, and revolutionary socialism. She sought to demonstrate that the Arab "nation" could achieve these three great objectives only by submitting to Egyptian guidance.

The origins, nature, and thrust of Egyptian imperialism have been shaped by the interplay of internal and external factors. A grandiose foreign policy affords Egypt's leaders an escape from the necessity of confronting insoluble domestic economic problems. Successes in the international arena overshadow failures in the domestic one. A rousing foreign policy accords the impoverished Egyptian masses a means of vicarious gratification. At the same time, such a foreign policy provides the charismatic leader with protection from disaffection and revolt among the military, by surrounding the leader with an aura of unique greatness and by providing the military with the expensive weapons and the social prestige it craves.

External factors have also played a major role in the development of Egyptian imperialism. If power abhors a vacuum, then the Middle East after World War II provided a perfect setting for the unfolding and conflict of rival imperial ambitions. The withdrawal of Britain and France in the 1940s left a vacuum which Egypt, Israel, the United States, and the Soviet Union hastened to fill. Among the Arab states the obvious disparity in population and strength between Egypt, on the one hand, and any of the other Arab states, on the other, naturally served to tempt Egypt to embark upon a forward policy. A political consideration—the desire to prevent the emergence of a unified Syrian-Iraqi state which could frustrate Egypt's ambitions—and an ideological one—the desire to overthrow reactionary monarchical regimes—also contributed to Nasser's decision to resume Farouk's hegemonic policy after 1954. The vanity of Egyptian statesmen and the contemptuous attitude of the Egyptian people toward the other Arabs have encouraged a forward policy from 1945 to the present.

Egypt has relied upon a panoply of devices to implement its hegemonic policy: military intervention, subversion, fostering the accession to power of client groups within other Arab states, the generation and management of Arab unity drives, preventive action to deny antagonistic states the opportunity of increasing their power through unopposed expansion, propaganda, and the attempt to manipulate the Arab-Israeli conflict to serve Egyptian ends.

Egyptian imperialism does not derive from ideological wellsprings. Nasser and his successors have had greater difficulty with their ideological confreres in Syria and Iraq than with their ideological adversaries in Saudi Arabia and Jordan. Nasser manifested a total disregard for such considerations during the period of union with Syria. Thus, despite the fact that it was the ideologically akin *Ba'th* which played a crucial role in bringing about the establishment of the United Arab Republic in 1958, Nasser elbowed it aside as soon as the union was established.

The outstanding fact about Egyptian imperialism since 1945 has been its utter failure. Nasser's two greatest efforts, the union with Syria (1958–61), and Egypt's intervention in Yemen (1962–67) were both fruitless. Even when ideologically and politically hostile royalist regimes were overthrown Nasser gained little. The destruction of the hated Hashemite monarchy in Iraq in 1958, for example, was followed not by an improvement in Egyptian-Iraqi relations but by further deterioration. Egypt at the time of Nasser's death exercised no greater control over the policies of the other Arab states and enjoyed no more real deference from them than she had during the reign of King Farouk.

Between 1957 and 1967 Nasser devoted his efforts to fostering Egypt's bid for hegemony within the Arab world. The Egyptian leader's behavior during this period suggests that a fundamental compatibility exists between Egypt's intra-Arab hegemonic ambitions and Israel's policy of limited imperialism.

The 1967 war was an unmitigated disaster for Egypt. Any prospect she had of realizing her ambitions within the Arab world was destroyed, along with her army and her prestige, in the June war.

The existence of a powerful Israeli state has, from the outset, doomed the aspirations of an anti-Israeli Egypt. Besides geographically interposing itself between Egypt and the Arab states of western Asia, Israel has prevented Egypt from obtaining control over Jordan. The knowledge that Israel would, in the end, intervene militarily to prevent the

unification of the Arab states under Egyptian leadership has, in the final analysis, made this ambition
impossible of realization, were Egypt to surmount
all other obstacles. Beyond this, Egypt has, as a
condition of its aspiration to primacy within the
Arab world, felt constrained to champion the cause
of the Palestinians against the formidable state of
Israel. Egypt, rather than controlling the foreign
policies of other Arab states has, as a consequence
of its acceptance of this obligation, found that it has
in fact placed Egyptian foreign policy at the mercy
of hostile elements within the Arab world. The
ultimate result has been disastrous for Egypt.

The decision to undertake leadership of the struggle against Israel has generated strong pressure
upon Egypt to stifle, at least during periods of tension between Israel and the Arab states, its differences with fellow Arab states. Egypt has, in other
words, been compelled to hold in abeyance actions
which would conduce to the realization of its intra-
Arab hegemonic aspirations. She has always been
and must always remain the loser in the contest to
be more anti-Israel than the other Arab states. For
to win a clear-cut victory in this competition, she
must inevitably run the risk of a dangerous confrontation with a fearsome antagonist.

The ideal scenario for Egypt would be for her
to unite the Arab states under her leadership, defeat
Israel, and then subordinate the Arab world to her
will. In view of the demonstrated impossibility of
achieving even the first stage of this program, the
second best course for Egypt would be to come to
terms with Israel and, with Israeli sanction and support, acquire hegemony within the Arab world.[1]

[1] It should be noted that even were Egypt to successfully
carry out the first two stages of this program, the cost to

The futility of Egypt's policy of seeking to attain its intra-Arab ambitions by shouldering the burden of leading the anti-Israeli effort is eloquently attested to by the fact that three conservative Arab monarchies—Kuwait, Saudi Arabia, and Libya (pre-'69)—found it advantageous to subsidize Egypt after the 1967 war, making continued Egyptian antagonism toward Israel the condition for the maintenance of this subvention. These states recognized that as long as Egypt's energies were engaged in the struggle against Israel she would be unable to concentrate her resources against her enemies within the Arab world.

The 1967 war cost Egypt territory of very considerable strategic and economic value. It compelled her to withdraw her military forces from Yemen, and thus terminate a costly effort with little to show for her exertions. Egypt's failure in the war also left her in a position of dependence vis-à-vis other Arab states.

Egypt has suffered grievously by allowing the condition for Arab primacy to be defined as leadership in the struggle against Israel. After the 1956 war, Nasser fully appreciated the risks which such a role entailed. He consequently went to great lengths to avoid a confrontation with Israel. In the end though, unable to control the Palestinian guerrillas and the extremist Syrian government, he was forced in 1967 to make a crucial decision. The Egyptian leader opted for the conventional policy: he would attempt to deter Israel, despite the obvious risks of such a policy, rather than surrender Egypt's

---

Egypt, against whom the Israelis would undoubtedly deploy the bulk of their military strength, would be prohibitive. The end result might well be that another Arab state would step in to reap the fruits of Egypt's efforts.

claim to preeminence in the Arab world. This course, needless to say, was catastrophic for Egyptian ambitions.

What Nasser did not consider in 1967, what was unacceptable then, was a third course which, in fact, has more to commend itself to Egypt than either of the alternatives. A unilateral Egyptian settlement with Israel would liberate Egypt from the impossible burden of having to confront the invincible Israeli power. Egypt, acting with Israeli approval and benefiting from Israeli subsidies, would be able to act decisively against her Arab antagonists. Realizing her ambitions for supremacy within the Arab world under the aegis of an Israeli suzerain would be far more satisfying for Egypt than persisting in her vain opposition to Israel without any prospect of recovering her lost territory, not to mention achieving her hegemonic ambitions. Such a strategy would free Egypt from her current dependence on the oil-rich states of the Middle East and would end the ignominy of placing Egyptian foreign policy at the mercy of weaker parties (Syria, and the Palestinian guerrilla organizations). Egypt would also obviate the danger that a rival Arab state would settle with Israel and accept the position Egypt could otherwise have for itself.

Egypt would benefit from a relationship with Israel, in which she would serve as overlord of the Arab states under overall Israeli supervision, in that she would be able, as a consequence of her emancipation from fear of Israeli attack, to dispense with the uncomfortable Soviet "protector" permanently. The withdrawal of the Soviets would liberate Egypt from the ever-present danger of satellitization. With the eventual revision of Soviet objectives in the Middle East, and the Soviet Union's ultimate departure from the region, the principal prop supporting the radical Arab states would be removed. With complementary adjustments in the policy of the United States (which would be happy to accept the de facto neutralization of a region which has been transformed into a virtual Soviet sphere of influence, and which would be pleased to resume economic and other aid to Egypt as part of the new design), the chief bulwark of the conservative Arab states would be eliminated and Egypt would be able to bring her enhanced assets to bear against these traditional opponents without fear of American intervention.

The conflict between Israeli imperialism and Egyptian imperialism is obvious. But this conflict is superficial over the near and intermediate term, and possibly over the long term as well. The compatibility of the two imperialisms stems from differences in direction, scope of ambition, and military capability. Egypt is primarily interested in acquiring a preponderant position within the Arab world. Israel, because of its western orientation, its ethnocentrism, the structure of its economy, and the nature of its political institutions and ideals, has little interest in acquiring the kind of position Egypt seeks. Israel's principal concern is the preservation of its territorial integrity. Egypt's interest in destroying the state of Israel has always been a strictly secondary and long-term objective, if that. Egypt wants, and as overseer of the Arab world under overall Israeli supervision is likely to continue to lack, the military power necessary to jeopardize the security of Israel. An Egypt which accepts a position of vassalage to Israel could, besides realizing its principal ambition, still hope to ultimately settle accounts with Israel.[2]

The development of an imperial relationship between Israel and Egypt would be eminently satisfactory to Israel. Israel would, as a consequence, be relieved of the perpetual anxiety and insecurity which she is now constrained to endure. Her borders would become secure. The ultimate danger of obliteration at the hands of a hostile Egypt which has succeeded by one means or another in acquiring nuclear weapons would be avoided. The economic subsidization and political promotion of Egypt would be far less costly than the maintenance of an enormous military establishment. The threat to the democratic institutions of the state which the existence of a garrison state and a siege mentality ineluctably creates would be dissipated. Israeli prestige would grow enormously as Israel came to occupy an eminent and generally accepted place within the Middle Eastern international system of complementary imbalances (Israeli-Egyptian and Egyptian-Arab). Finally, it is likely that this ironical reversal of history, which would see Israel move from the role of vassal state to that of imperial suzerain, and as such progenitor of the Egyptian empire, would be far more gratifying to her than continuing to prevent the emergence of such an empire by a futile "divide to defend" policy among the Arab states.

There would, of course, be a danger involved in the policy of patronizing an emergent Egyptian imperialism. Egypt might, in time, become so power-

[2] Defeating Israel and establishing Egyptian ascendancy in the Arab world under Soviet suzerainty would be no more of a success for Egyptian foreign policy than establishing Egyptian preponderance in the Arab world under overall Israeli hegemony.

ful that she would be able to turn on Israel and destroy the Jewish state. Yet all policies entail risks, and the theoretical possibility of this occurring is insufficient to negate the appeal of a course which stands an excellent chance of being legitimized within Egypt and the Arab world. Israel's present course is costlier, less productive, and more uncertain in outcome than the policy of sponsoring and manipulating Egyptian imperialism is likely to be. In the event that Egypt was apparently becoming dangerously powerful, and no new struggle emerged to supersede the Arab-Israeli conflict and thus render it irrelevant, Israel could take preventive action, either directly or indirectly, by subsidizing and protecting the concurrently rising opposition to Egypt's preponderance. Israel could, by recourse to this latter technique, maintain a favorable balance of power in the Middle East without herself having to do any more than a bare minimum of the actual fighting.

The likely future evolution of the Israel-Egyptian struggle, which we have considered in the above paragraphs, should prove highly attractive to the superpowers. Both the U.S. and the U.S.S.R. have every incentive to withdraw from the Middle East. The overriding interest of both superpowers is the same: avoidance of nuclear war. As long as the United States and the Soviet Union remain deeply involved in the Middle East as arm suppliers, imperial benefactors, and political guarantors of rival client states there is always the danger that the festering conflict between Israel and the Arab states will erupt into large-scale violence once again, with the attendant danger of escalation into an unwanted U.S.-Soviet confrontation. The support and sponsorship by the United States and the Soviet Union of rival client states within the Middle East is clearly out of harmony with the detente which the two powers have made the basis of their relations. Apart from the fact that this involvement threatens far greater interests than those it can conceivably be expected to promote in a conventional balance of power sense, it is especially unproductive of meaningful results in view of the fundamentally changed basis of security in the nuclear age, however insecure. It is apt to move toward a more "even-handed" policy respecting the U.S. and the U.S.S.R., compensating the Soviet Union for any "loss" in the Arab world without prejudice to any *real* American interest.

Against the very limited gains which success in the Middle East can generate, the superpowers must consider growing counterpressures against international involvements of this sort emanating from their own societies. Within the United States there is a rising tide of disenchantment with America's imperial policy or, at the very least, with the cost and apparent futility of conducting such a policy without reliable regional surrogates to bear the brunt of the burden. At the same time there persists among the policymaking elite and among the public at large an unwillingness to accept a severe diminution of American prestige by abruptly terminating expensive and apparently unsuccessful involvements. These considerations apply to the Middle East as much as to Southeast Asia. (As does the foreign policy elite's reluctance, by and large, to abandon the conventional balance of power approach to international politics.)

All of these problems would be satisfactorily resolved for the United States by a mutual U.S.-Soviet withdrawal from the Middle East, *pari passu* with the crystallization of an Israeli-Egyptian understanding along the lines sketched out earlier. America's interests, even when conceived of as a function of the balance of power, would be more efficaciously promoted through the establishment of Israeli suzerainty over a subhegemonic Egypt than via the more traditional method of attempting to separate the moderate Arab states from the radical ones, and thereby implement the timeless policy of *divide et impera*. In view of the demonstrated impossibility of putting the Israeli-Arab conflict into cold storage, and in view of the impossibility of creating a *modus vivendi* within the Middle East without a fundamental restructuring of attitudes, which can in turn result only from a substantially changed configuration of power within the region, the desirability, from the American viewpoint, of an evolution of the sort we have discussed here is obvious.

The Soviet Union, like the United States, has good reason for seeking to extricate itself from the Middle East. Besides the overriding Soviet interest in avoiding a confrontation with the United States, the U.S.S.R. must concentrate its scarce resources upon the evolving conflict with China. In addition, the Soviet regime must meet, at least in part, growing pressures within Soviet society itself for an increase in the production of consumer goods.

While Soviet policy in the Middle East, when judged by the standards of conventional diplomacy, has been highly successful (at least until the recent expulsion of Soviet personnel from Egypt), serious question has arisen as to the durability of Soviet gains after enormous financial outlays. If the Soviets stress their reluctance to terminate their involvement in the Middle East, as they are indeed likely to do for bargaining reasons, the United States might offer them compensation for the advantages they will be giving up in agreeing to a joint U.S.-Soviet withdrawal. Compensation might be in the area of trade, or might possibly involve some symbolic concessions to the Soviet Union in Europe.

The reorganization of Middle Eastern international politics along the lines of an inter-imperial relationship between Israel and Egypt is still some years in the future. But there are already signs that the evolution toward such a changed structure of relations is underway. Nasser, in the wake of the 1967 debacle, indicated that he had come to accept the idea that a settlement in which Egypt would adopt a policy of peaceful coexistence with Israel in exchange for a return of the occupied territories was desirable for Egypt. The conclusion of an agreement embodying these points, or some variation of them, would have constituted a first step in the evolution of Israeli-Egyptian relations. Nasser had been in the process of jettisoning Egypt's long-standing policy of leading the anti-Israel coalition in favor of a policy of accommodation in the last years of his life. His death brought a temporary halt to these promising developments. But the thread will in all probability be picked up again, if for no other reason than the lack of any viable alternative for Egypt. Coexistence was succeeded by detente in the history of postwar U.S.-Soviet relations, and detente is currently in the process of being superseded by entente between the two superpowers. There is no sufficient reason why this pattern of development should not be repeated in the case of Israeli-Egyptian relations, if only the temporal perspectives of a 'definitive' settlement are sufficiently extended to make up for the constriction of space and sentiment which prevents it in the short run.

The natural course of Egyptian-Israeli relations after the establishment of the state of Israel would have been armed conflict between Egypt, the most populous and strongest of the Arab states, and Israel, the other leading power within the Middle East. This struggle would normally have culminated in a decisive victory for one and defeat for the other, with the loser suffering either obliteration or clientalization. Although Israel achieved conclusive military triumphs on three occasions subsequent to the establishment of the state, the natural consequences of these victories were not realized in either 1949 or 1957 because of the intervention of outside powers. In 1967, although there was still a sufficient degree of great power interference to prevent Israel from translating its military success into a favorable political settlement, thereby ending the artificially prolonged Israeli-Egyptian conflict, Israel did achieve sufficient success to induce Egypt to adjust to its ascendancy if the terms were right in the short run and face-saving in the long run. This process was underway at the time of Nasser's death. After a period of confusion in post-Nasser Egypt, it will in all likelihood be resumed.

BIBLIOGRAPHY

A Note on Sources

I have used many secondary works, but have relied upon primary sources wherever possible. In particular, I have utilized diaries, memoirs, speeches, Zionist tracts, and state papers.

More specifically, the following sources have been used: the diaries of Theodor Herzl and Moshe Dayan; the memoirs of Zionist leaders and statesmen—Chaim and Vera Weizmann, David Ben-Gurion, Stephen Wise, Abba Hillel Silver, Frederick Kisch, Zeev Sharef, Walter Eytan, and David Horowitz; the memoirs of Jewish terrorists—Menachem Begin, Geula Cohen, and Doris Katz; the memoirs of British officers and officials—Sir John Bagot Glubb, Richard Graves, Richard Meinertzhagen, Anthony Nutting, and Sir Ronald Storrs; the reminiscences of U.N. officials—Pablo de Azcarate, Folke Bernadotte, General Burns, Jorge Garcia-Granados, and E. H. Hutchison; and the memoirs of such sundry figures as Norman Bentwich, Richard Crossman, Bartley Crum, Elias Epstein, James G. McDonald, Munya Mardor, and Erwin Rosenberger; the speeches of Theodor Herzl, Chaim Weizmann, Moshe Sharett, Levi Eshkol, Golda Meir, and Abba Eban; the Zionist tracts of Moses Hess, Leo Pinsker, Herzl, A. D. Gordon, Asher Ginzberg, Henrietta Szold, Israel Cohen, and David Ben-Gurion; and state papers—the Report of the Anglo-American Committee of Inquiry, reports of the British government on conditions in Palestine, and statements of policy (White Papers) issued by the British government during the mandatory period.

143

Principal Background Sources

For the Zionist thought of Moses Hess, the philosopher's *Rome and Jerusalem* is indispensable. An interesting commentary on Hess's ideas is provided by Sir Isaiah Berlin, *The Life and Opinions of Moses Hess.* Mary Schulman, *Moses Hess: Prophet of Zionism,* is also of interest.

The principal source for Leo Pinsker's ideas is the Russian Zionist's *Auto-Emancipation.* For background information regarding the etiology of Pinsker's ideas, Asher Ginzberg's *Pinsker and His Brochure* is useful.

For the principal ideas of Theodor Herzl, *The Jewish State* and *Old-New Land* are indispensable. Herzl's *Congress Addresses* and his statement to the British Royal Commission in 1902 contain an important statement of his ideas, and also present the case for Zionism. The *Complete Diaries of Theodor Herzl* are invaluable for the insight they afford into the development of Herzl's thought, and for their frank explication of his diplomatic strategy and his conception of the dynamics of international politics.

A number of biographies cast additional light upon Herzl and his ideas, policies, and diplomatic tactics. Of particular interest are Oscar K. Rabinowicz, *Herzl, Architect of the Balfour Declaration,* who examines Herzl's diplomatic and political efforts in Britain; Erwin Rosenberger's memoir, *Herzl As I Remember Him;* Alex Bein, *Theodor Herzl;* Joseph Adler, *The Herzl Paradox;* Nina Brown Baker, *Next Year in Jerusalem;* Jacob De Haas, *Theodor Herzl: A Biographical Study;* Josef Fraenkel, *Theodor Herzl: A Biography;* Emanuel Neumann, *The Birth of Jewish Statesmanship: The Story of Theo-*

dor Herzl's Life; Joseph Patai, *Star Over Jordan: The Life and Calling of Theodor Herzl;* and Ludwig Lewisohn, editor, *Theodor Herzl: A Portrait For This Age.*

The ideas of the principal Zionist thinkers are scrutinized in Ben Halpern's admirable *The Idea of the Jewish State,* and in Barnet Litvinoff, *The Road to Jerusalem.* Richard Gottheil's *Zionism* furnishes a competent history of Zionist efforts in the nineteenth and early twentieth centuries, as well as a recounting of the ideas of the leading nineteenth-century Zionist thinkers.

Alex Bein, *Return to the Soil,* provides a worthwhile study of the growth of the Zionist settlement in Palestine from the latter decades of the nineteenth century onward.

Bibliographical Note

Chapter I. A Note on the Foreign Policy of the Ancient Jewish Kingdoms of Judah and Israel

The most reliable, comprehensive, and up-to-date scholarly source for ancient Jewish history is volume I of Simon M. Dubnov, *History of the Jews.*

Chapter II. Zionist Foreign Policy during the Period of the British Mandate

Leonard Stein, *The Balfour Declaration,* offers a thorough, highly detailed study of Zionist diplomatic efforts to procure a pro-Zionist declaration from Great Britain. For the essence of the Anglo-Zionist agreement, see David Lloyd George, *The Truth About the Peace Treaties,* volume II.

Weizmann's autobiography, *Trial and Error,* is

indispensable, both for his ideas, perceptions, and strategy, and for its inside chronicle of Zionist diplomatic and political activities from World War I to the establishment of the state of Israel. Weizmann's *American Addresses, Excerpts from His Historic Writings and Addresses, Extracts from His Speeches on the Keren Hayesod,* and *Statement Made before the Palestine Royal Commission in Jerusalem on November 25, 1936,* provide additional insights into his thinking. They also present the Zionist case as developed during the mandatory period. Ben Halpern, *The Idea of the Jewish State,* makes a number of interesting points about Weizmann's ideas. For additional material on Weizmann, see Leonard Stein, *Weizmann and England;* and Meyer W. Weisgal, editor, *Chaim Weizmann: Statesman, Scientist, Builder of the Jewish Commonwealth.*

Frederick Kisch, *Palestine Diary,* is useful for the Zionist case during the mandate, for insight into the objectives of the Zionist movement, and for the Zionist leadership's perceptions of the British role in bringing about the deterioration of Arab-Jewish relations and the necessity of military self-help. For the state of mind of the *Yishuv* during the mandate, see Elias M. Epstein, *Jerusalem Correspondent 1919–1958.* Richard Meinertzhagen, *Middle East Diary 1917–1956,* is the invaluable memoir of a strongly pro-Zionist British officer. Meinertzhagen's early understanding of the inevitability of Arab-Jewish conflict in view of the irreconcilability of their political objectives, and his advocacy of an Anglo-Zionist alliance in view of the likely future politico-military weakness of the Arabs, are striking. David Ben-Gurion, *The Jews in Their Land,* is useful for this leading Zionist's understanding of the necessity for military self-help in view of the unreliability of the great power guarantor. Ben-Gurion, *Israel: Years of Challenge,* should be consulted for Ben-Gurion's assessment of the political situation in Palestine during the mandate, for his conception of the nature of interstate relations, and for the approach he believed the Zionists ought to follow with regard to their relations with the Arabs. In *Test of Fulfillment: Can It Be Achieved?,* Ben-Gurion presents the standard case for Zionism.

Palestine, Report on Immigration, Land Settlement and Development, Command 3686, by John Hope Simpson, *Palestine Royal Commission Report, Command 6019,* and *Report of the Commission on the Palestine Disturbances of August, 1929, Command 3530,* are valuable for their forceful statement of the Arab case. *The Memoirs of Sir Ronald Storrs* is similarly sympathetic to the Arabs, and should be consulted for Storrs's explanation of Arab antagonism toward Zionism. George Antonius, *The Arab Awakening,* contains a statement of the Arab case by an important Arab intellectual. Norman and Helen Bentwich, *Mandate Memories 1918–1948,* casts additional light upon the situation within the *Yishuv* during the 1920s and 1930s, especially with respect to Jewish attitudes toward the Arabs, Jewish-Arab relations, and Zionist introversion.

Esco Foundation, *Palestine: A Study of Jewish, Arab and British Policies,* provides a comprehensive treatment of the policies and attitudes of the three protagonists during the mandatory period. Jacob C. Hurewitz, *The Struggle for Palestine,* is an excellent history of the Jewish-Arab confrontation in Palestine during the period of the British mandate. Albert M. Hyamson, *Palestine under the Mandate: 1920–1948* throws light on various aspects of the period, including relations between the Diaspora and the *Yishuv*. Barnet Litvinoff, *The Road to Jerusalem*, should be consulted for Zionist policy during the mandatory period, and for the development of the *Yishuv*. Arthur Koestler, *Promise and Fulfillment*, is useful for its description of the *Yishuv's* policy and attitude toward the Arabs. John Marlowe, *The Seat of Pilate*, a somewhat anti-Zionist history of the mandatory period, with an emphasis upon the British role in Palestine, is of some value. Stephen Wise and Jacob De Haas, *The Great Betrayal*, is useful for the Zionist sense of betrayal at the hands of Britain. Joseph B. Schechtman, *The Vladimir Jabotinsky Story* is of great value for Jabotinsky's ideas.

Chapter III. The Independence Period

David Ben-Gurion, *The Jews in Their Land*, and *Test of Fulfillment: Can It Be Achieved?*, are essential for Ben-Gurion's fundamental ideas in the independence period, and for Zionist objectives and perceptions. Robert St. John, *Ben-Gurion,* provides a useful chronicle of Ben-Gurion's activities in the independence period, as well as speculations regarding the motivations underlying his important decisions. David Horowitz, *State in the Making*, is also useful for Zionist perceptions, attitudes, and the *Yishuv's* state of mind after World War II. Jon and David Kimche, *A Clash of Destinies*, and Arthur Koestler, *Promise and Fulfillment*, should be consulted for the calculations and reasoning of the leaders of the *Yishuv*, as well as for the diplomatic and military history of the 1945–49 period. For the official Zionist policy during the last decade of the mandate, and for Ben-Gurion's thinking and strategy, see David Ben-Gurion, *Israel: Years of Challenge*. For the thinking of the principal leaders of the *Yishuv* by a man in intimate contact with this elite, see Zeev Sharef, *Three Days*. For an interesting interpretation of the views of the Zionist leaders and the genesis of these views see Richard Meinertzhagen, *Middle East Diary 1917–1956*. Ben Halpern, *The Idea of the Jewish State,* is useful for its discussion of the views of the principal political factions within the *Yishuv*. Chaim Weizmann, *Presidential Address at the Twenty-Second Zionist Congress,* is a good source for Weizmann's ideas and perceptions and attitudes in the period following the end of World War II. Vera Weizmann, *The Impossible Takes Longer,* provides further insights into Weizmann's thinking during this period. For the principal ideas and diplomatic strategy of the Revisionist leader Vladimir Jabotinsky, see Vladimir Jabotinsky, *The War and the Jew*. For the terrorists' point of view, Menachem Begin, *The Revolt: Story of the Irgun,* is invaluable, despite the heavy interlarding of apologia and propaganda. Also see Doris Katz, *The Lady Was a Terrorist*. For the internal foreign policy debate within the *Yishuv* and the influence of the domestic political struggle within the *Yishuv* upon the foreign policy ultimately adopted by the official institutions of the Jewish community of Palestine, see Theodore Huebner and Carl Hermann Voss, *This Is Israel*. Also see Norman and Helen Bentwich, *Mandate Memories 1918–1948*.

For the failure of the American government to rescue any significant portion of European Jewry during the holocaust, Arthur D. Morse, *While Six Million Died,* is indispensable. For Zionist disappointment in America's failure, see Stephen S. Wise,

Challenging Years: The Autobiography of Stephen S. Wise. For the history of U.S.-Zionist relations during the final decade of the mandate, Joseph B. Schechtman, *The United States and the Jewish State Movement* is invaluable. For the pessimistic expectations of a leading American Zionist with respect to what the Zionist movement could expect from U.S. foreign policy after World War II, see Abba Hillel Silver, *Vision and Victory.* For accounts of American diplomacy toward the Palestine issue in the 1945–48 period, see Herbert Feis, *The Birth of Israel,* and Nadav Safran, *The United States and Israel.* For the attitude of American policymakers toward the Arab-Israeli conflict in 1948–49 and for American diplomatic activities during this period, the memoir of the American ambassador to Israel, James G. McDonald, *My Mission in Israel 1948–1951* is useful.

For the course of events in Palestine in 1947–48 by a first-hand observer, see Pablo de Azcarate, *Mission in Palestine: 1948–1952.* The diplomatic history of the independence period, as well as an analysis of the factors leading to the adoption of the Partition Resolution by the U.N., are presented in Jorge Garcia-Granados, *The Birth of Israel.* A fine overall history of the entire course of the Arab-Jewish conflict appears in Jacob C. Hurewitz, *The Struggle For Palestine.*

For a military history of the 1948 war, see Netanel Lorch, *The Edge of the Sword.* Walter Z. Laqueur, *The Soviet Union and the Middle East,* should be consulted for the motivations behind the Soviet Union's pro-Zionist stand in the 1947–48 period. For Arab expectations at the outset of the military struggle in 1948, see Sir John Bagot Glubb, *A Soldier with the Arabs.* For Arab intransigence in the independence period, see Folke Bernadotte, *To Jerusalem.* For an explanation of the mainsprings of Britain's anti-Zionist policy after World War II, Leonard Stein, *Weizmann and England,* is useful.

Chapter IV. Israeli Foreign Policy

Don Peretz, *Israel and the Palestine Arabs,* is an excellent study of Israeli attitudes and policy toward the refugees. David Ben-Gurion, *Israel: Years of Challenge,* is essential for Ben-Gurion's perceptions and for the reasoning behind his major foreign policy decisions through 1963. See also Maurice Edelman, *Ben-Gurion: A Political Biography,* for Ben-Gurion's foreign policy ideas. For the official position on Israel's goals, see David Ben-Gurion, *Israel: The Tasks Ahead.*

Walter Eytan, *The First Ten Years: A Diplomatic History of Israel,* should be consulted for the standard Israeli explanation of the persistence of the Arab-Israeli conflict and for a defense of Israeli foreign policy in the 1950s. Abba Eban, *The Security Situation in the Middle East,* should also be consulted for the Israeli apologia. Golda Meir, *This Is Our Strength: Selected Papers of Golda Meir,* provides the official Israeli interpretation of the 1956 crisis and war, as well as a justification of Israeli foreign policy in general. Earl Berger, *The Covenant and The Sword: Arab-Israeli Relations, 1948– 56,* is a useful history of Arab-Israeli relations from 1948 to 1956. Ernest Stock, *Israel on the Road to Sinai,* is invaluable for its contribution to an understanding of the internal debate over Israeli foreign policy in the early 1950s. Articles in, *Suez: Ten Years After,* Anthony Moncrieff, editor, deal with various facets of the 1956 war.

Moshe Dayan, *Diary of the Sinai Campaign,* is useful for Dayan's perceptions and for insights into his personality. Naphtali Lau-Lavie, *Moshe Dayan,* should be consulted for Dayan's principal ideas and attitudes. E. L. M. Burns, *Between Arab and Israeli,* provides a detailed history of the military aspect of the Arab-Israeli conflict in the 1950s. Levi Eshkol, *The State Papers of Levi Eshkol,* is useful for Eshkol's comments on various domestic problems and for his apologia for the 1967 war. Aubrey Hodes, *Dialogue with Ishmael: Israel's Future in the Middle East,* should be consulted for the author's comments on the impact of the dynamic struggle for power within Israel upon Israeli foreign policy, both before the 1967 war and after. A good chronology of the events leading up to the 1967 war is furnished in Walter Z. Laqueur, *The Road to War, 1967.* Laqueur also deals with the foreign policy debate within the Israel cabinet prior to the 1967 war and the temper of Israeli public opinion during the same period. See also Theodore Draper, *Israel and World Politics,* for the diplomacy of the period preceding the 1967 war. For a history of U.S.-Israeli relations, see Nadav Safran, *The United States and Israel.* For a sympathetic view of Arab fears of Israeli expansionism, see Uri Avnery, *Israel without Zionists.*

SELECTED BIBLIOGRAPHY

Background Material

Primary Sources

Herzl, Theodor. *The Complete Diaries of Theodor Herzl*. Edited by Raphael Patai. Translated from the German by Harry Zohn. 5 volumes. New York and London: Herzl Press and Thomas Yoseloff, 1960.

Herzl, Theodor. *The Congress Addresses of Theodor Herzl*. New York: Federation of American Zionists, 1917.

Herzl, Theodor. *The Jewish State*. New York: American Zionist Emergency Council, 1946.

Herzl, Theodor. *Old-New Land*. Translated from the German by Lotta Levensohn. New York: Bloch Publishing Co., 1960.

Herzl, Theodor. *The Tragedy of Jewish Immigration: Evidence Given before the British Royal Commission in 1902*. New York: Zionist Organization of America, 1920.

Hess, Moses. *Rome and Jerusalem*. New York: Philosophical Library, 1958.

Pinsker, Leo. *Auto-Emancipation*. Washington, D.C.: Zionist Organization of America, 1944.

Rosenberger, Erwin. *Herzl As I Remember Him*. New York: Herzl Press, 1959.

Zangwill, Israel. *The East African Question: Zionism and England's Offer*. New York: The Maccabaean Publishing Co., 1904.

Secondary Sources

Adler, Joseph. *The Herzl Paradox*. New York: Hadrian Press, 1962.

Baker, Nina Brown. *Next Year in Jerusalem*. New York: Harcourt, Brace & Co., Inc., 1950.

Bein, Alex. *Return to the Soil*. Translated from the Hebrew by Israel Schen. Jerusalem: Youth and Hechalutz Dept. of the Zionist Organization, 1952.

Bein, Alex. *Theodor Herzl*. Philadelphia: The Jewish Publication Society of America, 1940.

Berlin, Sir Isaiah. *The Life and Opinions of Moses Hess*. Cambridge: Wotleffer, 1957.

De Haas, Jacob. *Theodor Herzl: A Biographical Study*. Chicago and New York: The Leonard Company, 1927.

Dubnov, Simon M. *History of the Jews in Russia and Poland*. Translated from the Russian by Israel Friedlander. 3 volumes. Philadelphia: The Jewish Publication Society of America, 1916–1920.

Fraenkel, Josef. *Theodor Herzl: A Biography*. London: Ararat Publishing Society, Ltd., 1946.

Ginzberg, Asher. *Pinsker and His Brochure*. Translated from the Hebrew by Henrietta Szold. Baltimore: The Lord Baltimore Press., 1892.

Gottheil, Richard J. H. *Zionism*. Philadelphia: The Jewish Publication Society of America, 1914.

Halpern, Ben. *The Idea of the Jewish State*. Cambridge: Harvard University Press, 1961.

Lewisohn, Ludwig, editor. *Theodor Herzl: A Portrait for This Age*. Cleveland and New York: World Publishing Co., 1955.

Litvinoff, Barnet. *The Road to Jerusalem*. London: Weidenfeld and Nicolson, 1966.

Neumann, Emanuel. *The Birth of Jewish Statesmanship: The Story of Theodor Herzl's Life*. New York: Zionist Organization of America, 1940.

Patai, Josef. *Star Over Jordan: The Life and Calling of Theodore Herzl.* Translated from the Hungarian by Francis Magyar. New York: The Philosophical Library, 1946.

Rabinowicz, Oscar K. *Herzl, Architect of the Balfour Declaration.* New York: Herzl Press, 1958.

Schulman, Mary. *Moses Hess: Prophet of Zionism.* New York and London: Thomas Yoseloff, 1963.

Stein, Leonard. *The Balfour Declaration.* London: Vallentine-Mitchell, 1961.

Weisgal, Meyer W., editor. *Theodor Herzl: A Memorial.* New York: Zionist Organization of America, 1929.

Weiss, John. *Moses Hess, Utopian Socialist.* Detroit: Wayne State University Press, 1960.

CHAPTER I

Dubnov, Simon, M. *History of the Jews.* Translated from the Russian by Moshe Spiegel. 3 volumes. New York: Thomas Yoseloff, 1967.

CHAPTER II

Primary Sources

Ben-Gurion, David. *The Jews in Their Land.* Translated from the Hebrew by Mordechai Nurock and Misha Louvish. London: Aldus Books, 1966.

Ben-Gurion, David. *Test of Fulfillment: Can It Be Achieved?* New York: American Emergency Committee for Zionist Affairs, 1942.

Bentwich, Norman, and Bentwich, Helen. *Mandate Memories 1918–1948.* New York: Schocken Books, 1965.

Epstein, Elias M. *Jerusalem Correspondent 1919–1958.* Jerusalem: The Jerusalem Post Press, 1964.

Great Britain. *Correspondence with the Palestine Arab Commission and the Zionist Organization, Command 1700, June 1922.* London: His Majesty's Stationery Office, 1922.

Great Britain. *Palestine, Report on Immigration, Land Settlement and Development, Command 3686,* by John Hope Simpson. London: His Majesty's Stationery Office, 1930.

Great Britain. *Palestine Royal Commission Report, Command 5479.* London: His Majesty's Stationery Office, 1937.

Great Britain. *Palestine, Statement of Policy, Command 6019.* London: His Majesty's Stationery Office, 1939.

Great Britain. *Report of the Commission on the Palestine Disturbances of August, 1929, Command 3530.* London: His Majesty's Stationery Office, 1930.

Kisch, Frederick H. *Palestine Diary.* London: Victor Gollancz, Ltd., 1938.

Lloyd George, David. *The Truth About the Peace Treaties.* 2 volumes. London: Victor Gollancz, Ltd., 1938.

Meinertzhagen, Richard. *Middle East Diary 1917–1956.* London: Cresset Press, 1959.

Storrs, Sir Ronald. *The Memoirs of Sir Ronald Storrs.* New York: G. P. Putnam's Sons, 1937.

Weizmann, Chaim. *American Addresses.* New York: Palestine Foundation Fund, 1923.

Weizmann, Chaim. *Chaim Weizmann, Excerpts From His Historic Writings and Addresses: A Biography,* ed. by Sam E. Bloch. New York: Jewish Agency, American Section, 1962.

Weizmann, Chaim. *Dr. Chaim Weizmann, Builder of Facts: Extracts from His Speeches on the Keren Hayesod.* Jerusalem: Palestine Foundation Fund, 1952.

Weizmann, Chaim. *The Jewish People and Palestine: Statement Made before the Palestine Royal Commission in Jerusalem on November 25, 1936.* Jerusalem: The Zionist Organization, 1937.

Weizmann, Chaim. *The Letters and Papers of Chaim Weizmann.* Edited by Leonard Stein. London: Oxford University Press, 1968.

Weizmann, Chaim. *Trial and Error: The Autobiography of Chaim Weizmann.* New York: Harper & Row, 1949.

Secondary Sources

Andrews, Fannie Fern. *The Holy Land under Mandate.* 2 volumes. Boston and New York: Houghton-Mifflin Co., 1931.

Antonius, George. *The Arab Awakening.* Philadelphia: J. B. Lippincott Co., 1939.

Barbour, Nevill. *Nisi Dominus.* London: G. G. Harrap and Company, 1946.

Bein, Alex. *Return to the Soil.* Translated from the Hebrew by Israel Schen. Jerusalem: Youth and Hechalutz Dept. of the Zionist Organization, 1952.

Esco Foundation. *Palestine: A Study of Jewish, Arab and British Policies.* New Haven: Yale University Press, 1947.

Halpern, Ben. *The Idea of the Jewish State.* Cambridge: Harvard University Press, 1961.

Hurewitz, Jacob Coleman. *The Struggle For Palestine.* New York: W. W. Norton & Co., 1950.

Hyamson, Albert M. *Palestine under the Mandate: 1920–1948.* London: Methuen & Co., 1950.

Kann, Jacobus H. *Some Observations on the Policy of the Mandatory Government of Palestine with Regard to the Arab Attacks on the Jewish Population in August 1929.* The Hague: Martinus Nijhoff, 1930.

Koestler, Arthur. *Promise and Fulfillment.* New York: The Macmillan Co., 1949.

Litvinoff, Barnet. *The Road to Jerusalem.* London: Weidenfeld and Nicolson, 1954.

Marlowe, John. *The Seat of Pilate.* London: Cresset Press, 1959.

Samuel, Maurice. *Harvest in the Desert.* Philadelphia: The Jewish Publication Society of America, 1944.

Schechtman, Joseph B. *The Vladimir Jabotinsky Story.* 2 volumes. New York and London: Thomas Yoseloff, 1956–61.

Stein, Leonard. *The Balfour Declaration.* London: Vallentine-Mitchell, 1961.

Stein, Leonard. *Weizmann and England.* London: W. H. Allen, 1966.

Weisgal, Meyer W., editor. *Chaim Weizmann: Statesman, Scientist, Builder of the Jewish Commonwealth.* New York: Dial Press, 1944.

Wise, Stephen S., and De Haas, Jacob. *The Great Betrayal.* New York: Brentano's, 1930.

CHAPTER III

Primary Sources

Anglo-American Committee of Inquiry. *Report to the United States Government and to His Majesty's Government in the United Kingdom.*

Washington: U.S. Government Printing Office, 1946.

Azcarate, Pablo de. *Mission in Palestine: 1948–1952*. Washington, D.C.: The Middle East Institute, 1966.

Begin, Menachem. *The Revolt: Story of the Irgun*. Translated from the Hebrew by Samuel Katz. Tel Aviv: Hadar Publishing Co., 1964.

Ben-Gurion, David. *Israel: The Tasks Ahead*. New York: Israel Office of Information, 1949.

Ben-Gurion, David. *Israel: Years of Challenge*. New York: Holt, Rinehart, & Winston, 1963.

Ben-Gurion, David. *The Jews in Their Land*. Translated from the Hebrew by Mordechai Nurock and Misha Louvish. London: Aldus Books, 1966.

Ben-Gurion, David. *Test of Fulfillment: Can It Be Achieved?* New York: American Emergency Committee for Zionist Affairs, 1942.

Bentwich, Norman, and Bentwich, Helen. *Mandate Memories 1918–1948*. New York: Schocken Books, 1965.

Bernadotte, Folke. *To Jerusalem*. Translated from the Swedish by Joan Bulman. London: Hodder and Stoughton, 1951.

Crum, Bartley C. *Behind the Silken Curtain: A Personal Account of Anglo-American Diplomacy in Palestine and the Middle East*. New York: Simon and Schuster, 1947.

Garcia-Granados, Jorge. *The Birth of Israel*. New York: Alfred A. Knopf, 1948.

Glubb, Sir John Bagot. *A Soldier With the Arabs*. London: Hodder and Stoughton, Ltd., 1957.

Horowitz, David. *State in the Making*. Translated from the Hebrew by Julian Meltzer. New York: Alfred A. Knopf, 1953.

Katz, Doris. *The Lady Was A Terrorist*. New York: Shiloni Publishers, 1953.

McDonald, James G. *My Mission in Israel 1948–1951*. New York: Simon and Schuster, 1951.

Meinertzhagen, Richard. *Middle East Diary 1917–1956*. London: Cresset Press, 1959.

Sharef, Zeev. *Three Days*. Translated from the Hebrew by Julian Meltzer. Garden City: Doubleday and Co., 1962.

Silver, Abba Hillel. *Vision and Victory*. New York: The Zionist Organization of America, 1949.

Truman, Harry S. *Memoirs*. 2 volumes. Garden City: Doubleday & Co., 1955.

Weizmann, Chaim. *Presidential Address at the Twenty-Second Zionist Congress*. Basle: The Jewish Agency for Palestine, 1946.

Weizmann, Chaim. *Trial and Error: The Autobiography of Chaim Weizmann*. New York: Harper & Row, 1949.

Weizmann, Vera. *The Impossible Takes Longer*. London: H. Hamilton, 1967.

Wise, Stephen S. *Challenging Years: The Autobiography of Stephen S. Wise*. New York: G. P. Putnam's Sons, 1949.

Secondary Sources

Feis, Herbert. *The Birth of Israel*. New York: W. W. Norton & Co., 1969.

Halpern, Ben. *The Idea of The Jewish State*. Cambridge: Harvard University Press, 1961.

Huebner, Theodore, and Voss, Carl Hermann. *This Is Israel*. New York: Philosophical Library, 1956.

Hurewitz, Jacob Coleman. *The Struggle for Palestine*. New York: W. W. Norton & Co., 1950.

Jabotinsky, Vladimir. *The War and the Jew*. New York: Dial Press, 1942.

Kimche, Jon, and Kimche, David. *A Clash of Destinies*. New York: Frederick A. Praeger, 1960.

Koestler, Arthur. *Promise and Fulfillment*. New York: The Macmillan Co., 1949.

Laqueur, Walter Z. *The Soviet Union and the Middle East*. New York: Frederick A. Praeger, 1959.

Lorch, Netanel. *The Edge of the Sword*. New York: G. P. Putnam's Sons, 1961.

Morse, Arthur D. *While Six Million Died*. New York: Random House, 1968.

Prittie, Terence. *Israel, Miracle in the Desert*. New York: Frederick A. Praeger, 1967.

Rosensaft, Menachem Z. *Moshe Sharett: Statesman of Israel*. New York: Shengold Publishers, 1966.

Safran, Nadav. *The United States and Israel*. Cambridge: Harvard University Press, 1963.

St. John, Robert. *Ben-Gurion*. Garden City: Doubleday and Co., 1959.

Schechtman, Joseph B. *The United States and the Jewish State Movement*. New York: Herzl Press, 1966.

Stein, Leonard. *Weizmann and England*. London: W. H. Allen, 1966.

Chapter IV

Primary Sources

Ben-Gurion, David. *Israel: Years of Challenge*. New York: Holt, Rinehart, & Winston, 1963.

Bentwich, Norman, and Bentwich, Helen. *Mandate Memories 1918–1948*. New York: Schocken Books, 1965.

Dayan, Moshe. *Diary of the Sinai Campaign.* Jerusalem, Tel Aviv, Haifa: Steimatzky's Agency, Ltd., 1965.

Eban, Abba. *The Security Situation in the Middle East.* New York: Israel Office of Information, 1953.

Eshkol, Levi. *The State Papers of Levi Eshkol.* Edited by Henry M. Christman. New York: Funk and Wagnalls, 1969.

Eytan, Walter. *The First Ten Years: A Diplomatic History of Israel.* New York: Simon and Schuster, 1958.

Horowitz, David. *State in the Making.* Translated from the Hebrew by Julian Meltzer. New York: Alfred A. Knopf, 1953.

Meir, Golda. *This Is Our Strength: Selected Papers of Golda Meir,* edited by Henry M. Christman. New York: The Macmillan Co., 1962.

Secondary Sources

Avnery, Uri. *Israel without Zionists.* New York: The Macmillan Co., 1968.

Berger, Earl. *The Covenant and the Sword: Arab-Israeli Relations, 1948–56.* London: Routledge & Kegan Paul, Ltd., 1965.

Burns, E. L. M. *Between Arab and Israeli.* New York: Ivan Oblensky, 1963.

Draper, Theodore. *Israel and World Politics.* New York: Viking Press, 1968.

Edelman, Maurice. *Ben-Gurion: A Political Biography.* London: Hodder and Stoughton, 1964.

Hodes, Aubrey. *Dialogue with Ishmael: Israel's Future in the Middle East.* New York: Funk and Wagnalls, 1968.

Laqueur, Walter Z. *The Road to War, 1967.* London: Weidenfeld & Nicolson, 1968.

Lau-Lavie, Naphtali. *Moshe Dayan.* London: Vallentine-Mitchell, 1968.

Moncrieff, Anthony, editor. *Suez: Ten Years After.* New York: Random House, 1967.

Peretz, Don. *Israel and the Palestine Arabs.* Washington: The Middle East Institute, 1958.

Safran, Nadav. *From War to War.* New York: Pegasus, 1969.

Safran, Nadav. *The United States and Israel.* Cambridge: Harvard University Press, 1963.

Stock, Ernest. *Israel on the Road to Sinai.* Ithaca: Cornell University Press, 1967.

Library of Congress Cataloging in Publication Data

Roberts, Samuel J.
    Survival or hegemony?

    (Studies in international affairs, no. 20)
    Bibliography: p.
    1. Israel—Foreign relations.
    2. Zionism—History.
    I. Title. II. Series: Washington Center of Foreign Policy
    Research. Studies in international affairs, no. 20.

DS119.6.R6   327.5694   73-8134
ISBN 0–8018–1541–X
ISBN 0–8018–1543–6 (pbk.)